Berlitz

Jamaica

Front cover: Dunn's River Falls

Right: a Rastafarian takes a break
in Black River

YS Falls • Fun for all at this tiered waterfall fringed by mature forest (page 73)

Blue Mountains • Explore the slopes of this magnificent mountain range on a guided walk (page 58)

Rose Hall Great House • Some believe that this landmark property, with its commanding coastal views, is haunted (page 32)

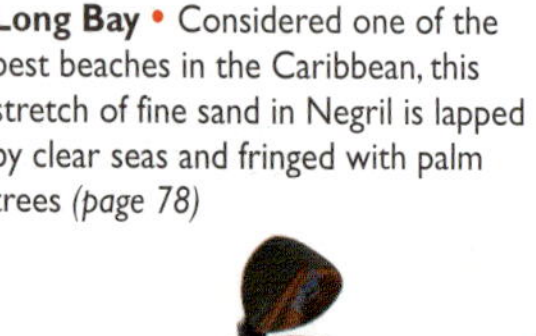

Long Bay • Considered one of the best beaches in the Caribbean, this stretch of fine sand in Negril is lapped by clear seas and fringed with palm trees (page 78)

The National Gallery • It features a large collection of Jamaican paintings and sculpture *(page 63)*

Runaway Bay • One of the most popular resorts on the north coast with good hotels and beaches *(page 38)*

Black River • Home to a variety of birds, fish and crocodiles *(page 74)*

Bob Marley Museum • A small but fascinating repository documenting the life and work of the reggae icon *(page 66)*

Treasure Beach • An ideal place for a relaxing getaway on the coast *(page 76)*

Dunn's River Falls • No visit to Jamaica is complete without a walk up these famous falls *(page 42)*

75

41

84

CONTENTS

Features

65

69

89

INTRODUCTION

The island of Jamaica amazed Christopher Columbus when he visited in 1494 on his second journey to the West Indies. He described it as the 'fairest island' and marvelled at the mountains that 'touched the sky'. Today's visitors will be equally charmed by the warm sunshine, beautiful beaches, rivers and streams that gush from ravines, lush tropical scenery and majestic mountains. However, since its history of diverse immigration has given rise to a vibrant grassroots culture, Jamaica is not just a holiday destination – it is also a rewarding cultural experience.

Landscape and Vegetation

The third-largest island in the Caribbean, just south of Cuba, Jamaica is 235km (146 miles) in length and 82km (51 miles) across at its widest point. The island is aligned almost east-to-west in the water so that sunrise wakes the eastern tip, proceeds to caress the length of the island, and kisses the western tip 'good night'. Geographically it is extremely diverse, with a central backbone of high mountains blanketed with a mixture of wet limestone forests and plantations of pine and native hardwood trees, such as mahoe and cedar. These are surrounded by areas of limestone formations, scrub and grassland, coral cliffs and fine sand beaches. Fresh water springs and tropical storms feed 120 rivers and some of the most celebrated waterfalls and cascades on earth.

On land, there is a wealth of animal and bird life. Rare species of butterflies and delicate hummingbirds take to the air, and crocodiles and a few manatees still live in and around large tracts of mangrove swamp in the south.

Boys fishing in Annotto Bay at sunset

The island is surrounded by coral reefs, which provide shelter for sea creatures and endless hours of recreation for divers and snorkellers.

Temperatures generally vary only a few degrees around 27°C (80°F), although the heat is tempered by the nearly continuous trade winds that blow across the Atlantic. In the mountains and hills of the interior, the temperature drops with altitude to as low as 3°C (37°F) on the mist-covered Blue Mountain Peak, the island's highest point at 2,256m (7,400ft).

Much of the land is extremely fertile and produces a range of tropical fruit and vegetable crops such as yams, sweet potatoes and juicy mangoes, providing ample food for the people, as well as cash crops such as bananas, sugar and coffee. Four hundred years ago these crops brought British colonists to rule the land and African slaves to work it, forever changing the landscape and the population.

Bananas: a cash crop

National Identity

Today's Jamaicans are a mixture of African and English people, with Spanish, Indian and a smattering of Portuguese, Jews, Chinese, Welsh and Irish. The cultures have melded together, giving rise to a fascinating national identity. Since independence in 1962, the black majority has worked to create a country based on confidence from within, working on a principle of pride in oneself and in one's

An artist in Ocho Rios

roots. This is so important for the future of the country that the national motto is 'Out of many – one people'.

Like most of the Caribbean islands, Jamaica was originally inhabited by Amerindians who had migrated from South America. The arrival of the Spanish at the end of the 15th century had a cataclysmic effect. Nowadays there is little evidence of the Castilian colonists, nor of the Amerindians they wiped out with their brutal slavery and European diseases – 160 years of Spanish rule have been blotted out by 307 years as a British colony.

Vestiges of the British colonial legacy can still be found, not least in the fact that English is Jamaica's official language: the popularity of cricket is another example. The 13 regional parishes and numerous towns were originally named after British settlements. You can find Manchester, Sheffield and Cambridge in Jamaica, to name but three. However, these British influences have, even from the earliest days of colonial rule, always been tempered and moulded to the Jamaican style. Jamaica has always had a second, 'unofficial' language developed from the early days of slavery. This creole, a mixture of English, African and Spanish words and phrases, is still evolving and is often indecipherable to the outsider. Next to town names derived from Spain and England, you'll also find names such as 'Wait Awhile' and 'Fruitful Vale', derived from the land and lifestyle of Jamaica.

The influence of the United States is now much stronger than that of Britain. Many Jamaicans head to the States for further education, and American economic influence continues to grow: the US dollar is accepted as readily as the Jamaican dollar to pay for goods.

However, Jamaica still revels in its own identity, which is now internationally recognised through such influential cultural products as the Rastafarian religion and reggae music. Rastafarianism originated in Jamaica in the 1930s and is still predominantly found here. Jamaican music – ska and, especially, reggae – has, since the 1970s, been exported and

Rastafarianism

One of the most popular images of Jamaica is that of the Rastafarian. His mane of dreadlocks and colourful 'tam' hat are instantly recognised worldwide. Rastafarians live by a series of strict rules. They are nonviolent and do not eat meat. Rastas use marijuana as an integral part of their religious experience and do not cut their hair, fearing the same loss of spiritual and physical strength that the biblical Samson experienced.

Members of the Rastafarian sect believe themselves to be one of the tribes of Israel, viewing the modern world as 'Babylon', synonymous with evil, and they seek peace with God, whom they believe is in all beings. Their spiritual leader is Haile Selassie, the late emperor of Ethiopia, who was God's messenger on earth – the 'Lion of Judah'.

Catamarans for rent, Negril

enjoyed around the world. The strong beat and earthy lyrics seem to symbolise and celebrate the character of this young and lively country.

Tourist Attractions

Since independence in 1962, tourism has become a major employer and source of income and the island is renowned as one of the top destinations in the Caribbean. While some of the hotels that attracted writers and film stars in the 1950s are still going strong as luxury hideaways, Jamaica has also pioneered the all-inclusive resort catering for the mass market. The best beaches are now home to some fine hotels and large resorts, aiming to supply everything you could need for the perfect vacation.

It is tempting, and possible, to spend your entire holiday in a resort. Yet to do this is to miss the very essence of what the island is all about. Once you step out of your hotel your

senses will be bombarded by a range of sights, sounds, smells, tastes and textures that are unique to Jamaica.

Break out of your all-inclusive resort for the chance to climb up or bathe in one of the many beautiful waterfalls, float down a lazy river on a raft, hike or bike through the forest surrounded by wildlife, or climb a mountain to watch the red glow of dawn.

Taste authentic Caribbean dishes such as *ackee* (a yellow vegetable) cooked with saltfish, Jamaica's national dish, and aromatic hot jerk pork cooked in a pit barbecue. Savour a freshly roasted and ground cup of Blue Mountain coffee or watch the sunset with a fine, aged Jamaican rum.

Hear the dance hall and reggae music booming from a hundred cranked-up car stereos or the chorus of tiny tree frogs that begins as evening

Jamaican handshake

The traditional Jamaican handshake – with clenched fists meeting first vertically then horizontally, after which the thumbs touch briefly – signals a parting of mutual understanding and respect.

descends. Feel the texture of a hand offered in greeting and try to get the hang of the Jamaican handshake. There's an abundance of nature, history, art and culture to be explored and enjoyed. Jamaica is an island with a strong personality that doesn't simply wait in the wings. It comes out to meet you.

A BRIEF HISTORY

The earliest signs of people on Jamaica are the remains of the Taino, Amerindians descending from Arawak-speaking people who migrated from the north coast of South America. They travelled to various Caribbean islands along the entire Antillean chain, arriving in Jamaica at the beginning of the eighth century.

The Tainos left an important legacy of rock paintings and carvings in places such as Runaway Caves near Discovery Bay, and shards of pottery found at their settlements near Sevilla la Nueva and Spanish Town have added a little to our knowledge about them. Over 200 Taino sites have been identified, and it is said that when the Spanish arrived in Jamaica there were approximately 100,000 Tainos living on the island. They called Jamaica *Xaymaca* ('land of wood and water').

Columbus and the Arrival of Europeans

Christopher Columbus first arrived in Jamaica on 5 May 1494. He stayed for only a few days but on his fourth voyage he spent a year stranded here in 1502–3, while his ships were being repaired. However, the island was not settled by the Spanish until 1509. The year before, Columbus's son Diego had been appointed Governor of the Indies by the Spanish monarchy and he made Juan de Esquivel Governor of Jamaica.

In 1510, Esquivel created a base called Sevilla la Nueva near St Ann's Bay, from which he hoped to colonise the rest of the island. The Spanish immediately began subjugating the native Arawak-speaking population, most of whom died under the yoke of oppression and of diseases carried by the Europeans.

Statue of Christopher Columbus, St Ann's Bay

The site of Sevilla la Nueva proved unhealthy and mosquito-ridden, and in 1534 the Spanish founded Villa de la Vega, today known as Spanish Town. Pig breeding was the main occupation of these early settlers, but they also planted sugar cane and other crops that required large numbers of labourers. The number of Taino had already fallen dramatically, so the Spanish began to import enslaved people from Africa to work the land; the first Africans arrived in 1517.

The island was never fully exploited by the Spanish. They were much more interested in the gold and other treasures to be found in South America. However, they had to protect the shipping lanes in order to get their treasure home, and this meant keeping hold of as much of the Caribbean (or the 'Spanish Main', as it was then known) as possible. They fortified the more strategic islands, but Jamaica was deemed less important than Cuba or Puerto Rico and, consequently, was poorly protected.

British Rule

In 1654 Oliver Cromwell, Lord Protector of England, dispatched a British fleet to the Caribbean to break the stranglehold of the Spanish. They were repulsed at Hispaniola by a strong Spanish force and decided to take Jamaica as a consolation prize. They sailed into what is now Kingston Bay in May 1655 and sent an ultimatum to the capital. The small Spanish force considered its position and decided to retreat, heading to the north coast and sailing to Cuba. Before they left, they freed their slaves, who fled into the interior of the island.

The Spanish attempted to retake the island in 1658 at the Battle of Rio Bueno but were defeated. Other European powers also began to put pressure on the defending forces and British naval power in the area was badly stretched. Sir Thomas Modyford, the Governor of Jamaica, offered a deal to pirate ships already well established in the area: if the pirates protected British assets, then they were free to harass enemy shipping with impunity. They agreed, and Modyford authorised the pirates to act in the name of the British Crown.

These 'privateers' were welcomed at Port Royal, the English settlement on the southern tip of Kingston harbour, and it quickly developed a reputation as the wickedest city in

The British flag flies in Kingston

the world. Plunder was now legitimate business and the city was awash with money and booty from the numerous pirate raids. There was little evidence of religion or of the rule of law. Henry Morgan was chief among the pirate leaders. He and his followers conducted a successful series of bloody raids on Spanish settlements in the Caribbean, culminating in the sacking of Panama, the major city of the Spanish Main.

In 1670 the Spanish officially ceded Jamaica to Britain as part of the Treaty of Madrid, and the British began a systematic process of settlement, offering land to prospective settlers. They rescinded their agreement with the privateers and began to evict them from Port Royal.

Henry Morgan was offered the post of Lieutenant Governor of the island and charged with driving out his former cohorts. The erstwhile pirate thus became a policeman during the last years of his life. Morgan died in 1688 before his task was complete, but nature finished what he had started: Jamaica suffered a powerful earthquake in 1692, and Port Royal sank into the sea, taking with it many of the treasures stolen from the Spanish.

The Lady Pirates

The pirates who sailed the Caribbean were joined by two women, Mary Read and Anne Bonney, who were said to be as ruthless as their compatriots. They dressed in men's clothing and committed unspeakable atrocities in the name of profit. Captured by the British authorities, they were found guilty of piracy and sentenced to death, but both pleaded 'the belly'. Judges would not kill an unborn child, so both sentences were commuted to life in jail. Mary Read and her young child died of fever only a few months later, but there is no record of what happened to Anne Bonney. Her life after the trial is a mystery.

Plantations and Slavery

As the 18th century began, trade in sugar cane and spices was becoming profitable. Plantation work was labour intensive, but there were few labourers on the island; the Spanish slaves had disappeared into the inhospitable interior with the few remaining Tainos. The decision was made to import a workforce from West Africa, resulting in some 600,000 enslaved Africans being transported to Jamaica over the next few decades. One in five slaves died en route and many more died of disease once on the island. On the back of this cruel system, Jamaica gradually became the biggest sugar producer in the world and a very wealthy island indeed.

Henry Morgan

Thirteen administrative parishes were created, forming the basis of government that we still see today. The Governor commissioned a representative (or custos) in each parish. Powerful land-owning families organised an Assembly to run the everyday affairs of the island, but many landowners continued to live in Britain, where they exerted tremendous influence in Parliament to protect their Jamaican interests.

Even in these early days there were slaves who fought against the tyranny of the system. The African slaves whom the Spanish had released after 1655 were known as Maroons, from the Spanish word *cimarrón* (which means 'wild' or 'untamed'). They made their settlements in the hills away from the British but began to attack colonists in a series of raids known as The First Maroon War. British forces suffered constant harassment at their hands and even named a part of the island 'The Land of Look Behind' in recognition of the surprise attacks they suffered. Eventually the British forced the Maroons into more isolated and remote pockets of land.

This war of attrition ended in 1739, when an agreement was reached between the two sides. The Maroons were allowed self-rule in designated areas in return for not helping escaped slaves. This agreement is at the root of Maroon self-government today. The plantation slaves also began organising revolts (the first in 1760), but their situation remained the same and they endured cruel and inhumane treatment.

During the American War of Independence, Jamaica came under threat again from other European powers, which saw Britain's problem to the north as a chance to capture its colonies in the Caribbean. Some islands were taken by the French, but Admiral Rodney saved Jamaica by defeating the French fleet at the Battle of Les Saintes in 1782. Jamaica thereafter became an island of strategic importance for the British, who based a large naval fleet at Fort Charles in Port Royal.

Emancipation

The French Revolution in 1789 sent ripples of discontent through the Caribbean. The French peasants' cry for freedom prompted another Maroon War on Jamaica, after which many Maroons were deported to Nova Scotia. There was, however, a growing abolition movement in Britain. In 1807 Parliament made the trade in slaves illegal, but the powerful sugar lobby ensured that slavery continued on the plantations. The enslaved people were angry and dispirited. Nonconformist churches en-

Rodney's riches

Following his decisive victory at the Battle of Les Saintes in 1782, Admiral George Rodney was honoured by the Crown with a barony and a pension of £2,000 a year.

Celebrating freedom

couraged the slaves to stand up and take action against injustice. Their intervention guaranteed the popularity of these Christian denominations; Baptist and Adventist churches are still as strong today as in the early 1800s.

The momentum for change was growing, and in 1831 a black lay preacher named 'Daddy' Sam Sharpe led a revolt of 20,000 slaves at Montego Bay. After a campaign of destruction, the authorities assured them that slavery would be abolished. Sharpe and approximately 1,000 other slaves surrendered peacefully, only to be rounded up and publicly executed. This news was met with revulsion in Britain and eventually led to full freedom in 1838.

Unfortunately, being 'free' solved none of the problems suffered by the population. There was no economic infrastructure outside the plantation system, and power remained in the hands of a small minority of white and mixed-race individuals. Meanwhile, Asian labourers took up the work previously carried out by the enslaved Africans; their descendants can still be found on the island, particularly around Little London in the west. As a further blow to the economy, the British Parliament passed the Sugar Equalisation Act in 1846 as part of a new free-trade policy. Jamaica's protected market was effectively gone.

In October 1865 at Morant Bay, there was another uprising, led by Baptist minister Paul Bogle and George Gordon, a mixed-heritage landowner. It brought savage retribution from the authorities, and both leaders were executed, but it prompted the dissolution of the Jamaica Assembly, which was dominated by plantation owners. The island became a Crown Colony ruled directly from London, and over the next few years there were several reforms to its political and social systems.

As the sugar trade declined in importance, economic disaster loomed. Fortuitously, another crop found favour with the industrial world: Jamaica became the island of bananas. The first consignments were exported in 1866 and, within a few years, thousands of tons were being shipped to markets in the US and Britain. The boats carrying the

Marcus Garvey – A National Hero

Born in St Ann's Bay in 1887, Marcus Mosiah Garvey made his mark as a black nationalist, instigating a 'back to Africa' movement. Garvey founded the Universal Negro Improvement Association (UNIA), advocating black unity and pride, and in 1916 he set up a UNIA office in New York. His political activities included the establishment of the Black Star Line steamship company and a newspaper, *The Negro World*, which became a forum for labour grievances. In 1925 Garvey was imprisoned for fraud on what are now considered false charges and later deported from the US. He died in obscurity in London in 1940, but after independence his remains were brought home to Jamaica, and he was inducted as a National Hero.

banana crops also fostered a fledgling tourist trade. The first visitors arrived as passengers on them, spending time around Port Antonio.

Still there was little change in conditions for the black majority, who had no economic or political power. The worldwide depression of the 1930s brought a new wave of demonstrations in Jamaica, and a number of individuals emerged to lead the people and pave the way for nationhood: Marcus Garvey

Marcus Garvey

called for black self-reliance; in 1938, Norman W. Manley founded the People's National Party (PNP), which found allies in the Jamaica Trades Union Congress and the National Workers Union; Manley's cousin, Sir Alexander Bustamante, formed the Industrial Trade Union and later (1944) the Jamaica Labour Party (JLP). Together, these organisations fought for local rule, which in 1944 resulted in universal voting rights for adults. At the same time, the early years of World War II brought American tourists who were no longer able to travel to Europe on holiday. Jamaica's popularity as a tourist destination was now undeniable.

Independence and Democratic Rule

In the postwar period there continued to be constitutional changes, including self-government for Jamaica in 1959. Britain hoped to create a Federation of Caribbean Islands in the region. Jamaica joined the West Indies Federation in 1958 but withdrew in 1961 following a national referendum.

Since independence in 1962, the political culture of Jamaica, which started out with such confidence and optimism, has been fraught with problems. Violence and corruption have been constant factors in the political process. From 1962 until 1972, the JLP held power. The party's broad aims were to support capitalist policies and to continue close ties with Britain and the rest of the Commonwealth.

In 1972, however, the left-wing PNP was elected with a massive majority. Michael Manley, son of Norman, led the party and pushed for policies that brought Jamaica closer to independent nonaligned countries. Manley was criticised for political links to Fidel Castro's Cuba, foreign investment dried up, wealthy Jamaicans left the island and the economy declined. The uncertain and volatile situation led to gang violence, and Jamaica seemed to be heading for civil war. In 1980 the JLP returned to power following a campaign that ended with hundreds dead. Foreign investment began to trickle back.

Politics Today

In 1989 the PNP regained power under Michael Manley, whose policies had changed radically (he now advocated the free market). From 1993, when Manley retired due to poor health, the PNP was led by Percival Patterson, Jamaica's longest serving Prime Minister. He was succeeded in 2006 by Portia Simpson-Miller, the party's first female leader. Her term of office was short-lived, however: the PNP was narrowly defeated in the 2007 elections by the JLP, led by Bruce Golding.

Veteran of the times in Kingston

Historical Landmarks

c. 700 Arawak-speaking Amerindians arrive on Jamaica from the Orinoco region of South America.

1494 Christopher Columbus lands on the north coast of Jamaica, claiming it for Spain.

1502–3 Columbus is stranded for a year near St Ann's following damage to his ships.

1510 First Spanish settlement founded at Sevilla la Nueva.

1517 First boat carrying African slaves arrives at the island.

1655 British forces take the island from the Spanish. The Spanish free slaves, who head to the interior of the island.

1670 The Treaty of Madrid cedes Jamaica to England.

1692 A powerful earthquake destroys the city of Port Royal.

1739 Peace treaty with freed slaves (Maroons), which offers them self-government.

1700s The number of African slaves increases dramatically, with around 250,000 working on Jamaican plantations.

1838 Emancipation of enslaved people.

1865 Morant Bay rebellion seeks better conditions for the liberated slaves. The ringleaders are executed.

1938 Difficult economic conditions lead to the formation of the first trade unions and political parties.

1944 Universal adult suffrage is introduced.

1962 Jamaica declares independence led by the JLP.

1972 Victory at the elections for the left wing Michael Manley and PNP.

1980 The JLP returns to power, led by Edward Seaga.

1989 Michael Manley returns to power with free market policies.

1993 P. J. Patterson of the PNP becomes Prime Minister.

1997 Michael Manley dies. The PNP return for a third term.

2006 P. J. Patterson retires. The PNP elects Portia Simpson-Miller as its first female leader and Jamaica's first female Prime Minister.

2007 After 18 years of PNP government, the JLP wins the elections and Bruce Golding becomes Prime Minister.

WHERE TO GO

The island of Jamaica is spectacularly beautiful, from its mountainous interior, lush forests and plentiful streams and rivers to the sandy beaches that frame the coast. You can kick back and relax on the seashore while admiring the view, or be more active and explore the wildlife at the bottom of a coral reef or at the top of a mountain peak. Wherever you go in Jamaica your senses will be bombarded by the sight of glorious landscapes, the pulsating bass tones of the music, the fragrance of brightly coloured tropical fruit and flowers, and the taste of spicy jerk meats and fish or a cold beer on a hot day.

In this chapter, we journey clockwise around the island, starting at the tourist capital of Montego Bay on the northwest coast. Sangster International airport is within relatively easy reach of all the main resort areas on the north and west coasts. Cruise ships also dock at the ports of Montego Bay and Ocho Rios.

The twisting roads of the rugged interior mean that cross-island journeys to Kingston and the south coast can take longer than expected, but a major road-building programme should soon change that. The North Coastal Highway and Highway 2000 in the south of the island will allow better connections between Kingston, Montego Bay and Ocho Rios. Parts of the North Coastal Highway are complete, such as the Negril–Montego Bay and Falmouth–Ocho Rios stretches. It is hoped that the Ocho Rios–Port Antonio leg will be finished soon.

Soon come

Switch to Jamaican time. The phrase 'Soon come' means that things will happen eventually. Don't be in a hurry for anything.

Rainbow over Blue Mountain

Fresh fruit for sale on the beach

MONTEGO BAY

The northern coast of the island has been the major focus of tourist development on Jamaica since the 1970s. Much of the burgeoning development has occurred here, and in some places this has changed the character of the landscape. However, there's no denying that this area has just about everything needed for a perfect holiday, whether you want to do nothing but sit on a beach, dive and snorkel along the coral reefs, enjoy sports, or explore the history and culture of the island.

Montego Bay, or 'MoBay' as it's called by the locals, is probably the most complete resort area in Jamaica, with its beaches, sports and shopping, along with a large number of hotels that cater to all budgets. The town is only minutes from the Sangster International airport (built as a US Air Force base during World War II), so there is no lengthy transfer to your hotel. The town is surrounded by a host of different sights and sporting facilities. Its disadvantage is a lack of attractiveness: Montego Bay is a rather soulless hodgepodge of sprawling development with no real character. But if you are here simply to have fun, you might not even notice.

Downtown

The resort sits on the east side of the wide bay, with the cruise port on the west. **Downtown Montego Bay** is located between the two. It is a jumble of loud and boisterous streets, full of people, dogs and goats breathing the fumes of hundreds of buses and cars. Vendors in makeshift shacks sell beer or cigarettes, and oil-barrel barbecues cook jerk chicken and burgers. The town centre is **Sam Sharpe Square**, previously called Charles Square and The Parade, but renamed after the hero of the 1831 slave rebellion who was hung for his part in the uprising. In one corner of the square are the **Cage**, an old prison lockup built in 1806 to house drunken sailors or runaway slaves, and the **Ring**, the site of

Samuel 'Daddy' Sharpe

Samuel 'Daddy' Sharpe (1801–32) was a literate slave and a lay preacher who lived on the Belvedere Estate, south of Montego Bay. Sharpe encouraged his congregation to lay down their tools until their grievances had been addressed. The resulting slave protest started peacefully at Christmas 1831, but turned violent. It was brutally suppressed, and Sharpe was executed on The Parade, now memorialised as Sam Sharpe Square. It has been argued that the reaction of the British public to the fate of the slaves and the rebellion's leaders led to parliamentary enquiries and the eventual emancipation of Jamaican slaves. Sharpe was honoured as a National Hero in 1975.

Local art, Montego Bay

the once-regular slave auction. The Civic Centre was redeveloped from the ruins of the 1804 court house. Inside is the **Museum of St James** (Tue–Fri 9am–5pm, Sat 10am–3pm, Sun noon–5pm; charge; www.stjamespc.org), which exhibits the history of the parish from the Tainos to the present day.

Nearby, **Fustic Street Craft Market** is a constant buzz of activity. This is the place to come to check out the range of local handicrafts and souvenirs. The windows and doors of over 100 wooden cabins are bedecked with printed sarongs, T-shirts and carved masks. Try your hand at haggling and you're bound to get a better price than you thought.

The Beaches

Head east to the **Gloucester Avenue** 'Hip Strip' for the beaches and resort life. This is the heart of the action, with some of the busiest bars, loudest music and wildest water sports on the island. As you reach Gloucester Avenue, you'll pass the remains of the **Fort Montego**, with its small sturdy walls and heavy cannon that guarded the bay for many years.

Most beaches in MoBay are private, which means you pay a small charge to enter. They are kept neat and tidy, with water sports facilities and areas for changing and showering. The first one along the strip is **Walter Fletcher Beach**, which is busy at weekends. The beach is home to **Aquasol Theme Park**, which offers loads of family fun and sports activities by day and has open-air dining and a disco in the evening (daily; charge; www.aquasoljamaica.com).

Further along the strip is **Doctor's Cave Beach**, the original Montego Bay beach developed in the Edwardian era when sea bathing became a popular pastime throughout the British Empire. It became a centre for wealthy and upper-class visitors and was donated to the town in 1906 by the original owner. It is still as popular as ever and the sand is sublime, but the cave after which the beach was originally named was destroyed in the early 1930s during a hurricane.

Cornwall Beach (daily 9am–5pm; charge), another private beach with perfect sand and sheltered waters, is behind the St James shopping mall. There is a bar, watersports and beach volleyball facilities.

The cruise port, or **Montego Bay Freeport**, sits on an outcrop on the west side of the bay. It is a popular stop on

Playing on the floating trampoline at Doctor's Cave Beach

Yachts moored at Montego Bay

cruise itineraries. This area is also home to the **Montego Bay Yacht Club**, which hosts a number of yachting regattas through the year. You can hire boats here to take a morning or full day out at sea for sport fishing or just a relaxing jaunt.

Montego Bay Marine Park (Howard Cooke Blvd; www.mbmp.or), established in 1992, covers the whole of Montego Bay from the high tide mark to a depth of 100m. It covers an area of 15.3 sq km (6 sq miles) of reef, sea-grass and mangrove swamps, stretching from Rum Bottle Bay in the west to Tropical Beach by the airport in the east. A number of companies offer underwater tours in glass-bottomed boats or submersible craft, or you can rent snorkel or scuba gear to get a closer look yourself. These can be booked from the offices at **Pier I**, a small marina with cafés and shops that sits in the middle of the bay between the beaches and the cruise port.

South of the Bay

South of Montego Bay there are a number of attractions that make enjoyable excursions, if you want to tear yourself away from the beach or book an outing from your cruise ship.

The **Barnett Estate** (daily; charge), with its 18th-century great house, has been owned by the Kerr-Jarrett family for over 250 years. Their ancestor Nicholas Jarrett arrived on the island in 1655, and the family was at the forefront of economic and political activities on Jamaica for many generations. They once owned almost all the land on which

Montego Bay now stands. You'll be able to tour the still-operating plantation and wander around the great house, which has been restored with many original touches.

Near the town of Anchovy, in the hills above Montego Bay, **Rocklands Bird Sanctuary** (daily 12.30–5.30pm; charge; no children under five years) offers a fascinating close-up encounter with the birds of Jamaica. The sanctuary began almost by accident in the late 1950s when founder Lisa Salmon (who died aged 96 in 2000) moved here. She loved the hummingbirds that inhabited the garden and began to feed them so that they became friendly. Sugar water for the hummingbirds and seed for finches and other birds are provided so that you can feed them.

High in the hills 27km (17 miles) south of Montego Bay is **Belvedere Estate** (Mon–Sat; charge). It is a working plantation producing a mixed crop of spices and fruits, but it also opens a fascinating window on plantation life during colonial times. The current owners have created an agricultural museum to demonstrate the traditional methods of crop production as well as everyday life on the plantation. The staff wear traditional clothing and work with the tools of their fore-fathers. You can even consult a traditional herbalist to cure your ailments.

En route, Anchovy

Rose Hall interior

EAST ON THE COAST ROAD

East along the main coast road from the Montego Bay area, there is a string of luxurious resort hotels with facilities such as golf courses and equestrian centres. Two shopping malls at Ironshore and Half Moon Resort have boutiques, gift shops and fast-food outlets. A number of sightseeing attractions lie along this route, which leads to Falmouth and, eventually, to Ocho Rios.

Great Houses

Rose Hall Great House (daily 9am–6pm; charge) is, perhaps, the most infamous house in Jamaica. Set high on a hill above the coast with commanding views, it was started in 1750 by George Ash and named after his wife Rose. The house was completed in 1777–80 by John Palmer, Rose's fourth husband. It was a calendar house, with 365 windows,

52 doors and 12 bedrooms. It later became the home of Annie Palmer when she married into the family; it is Annie who has given the house its fame and reputation. She was allegedly a white witch with potent voodoo powers who had murdered three husbands and an unidentified number of lovers before she herself died under mysterious circumstances. Locals, who believed that the house was haunted by her spirit, buried her nearby so that she could be reunited with her body and rest in peace. It is now believed that her behaviour could have been the result of lead poisoning, from eating her meals off lead plates.

The house fell into ruin after emancipation. In 1965 it was bought by the Rollins family, who renovated the main building. Rich mahogany wood cut from trees from the surrounding estate was used for new floors and ceilings. The interior has been redecorated with fabrics and furniture dating from the late 1700s to Victorian times. The ballroom has a woven wall-covering that is a reproduction of an original by Philipe de la Salle, which he created for Marie Antoinette.

Further east, **Greenwood Great House** (daily 9am–6pm; charge; www.greenwoodgreathouse.com) was once the property of one of the wealthiest and most powerful colonial families in Jamaica. The first Barrett family member came to the island with the invading English forces. His descendants were major landowners from the middle of the 16th century and played an important role throughout the colonial history of Jamaica, holding positions of great influence in the judi-

Rose Hall Great House

ciary and administrative bodies. Another member of the family was Elizabeth Barrett, who married poet Robert Browning. She was born in England and never came to the island: the responsibility for working the plantation lands fell to her male relatives.

This house, begun in 1780, was only one of the Barrett properties in the area and was built for entertaining rather than for use as a home. It survived the slave rebellions of the 1830s, unlike other plantation houses. The house belongs to the Betton family and has retained many original features and authentic touches. Furniture and art collected over the generations fills the house, but perhaps most fascinating is the collection of original musical instruments and machines used for entertainment before the advent of electricity. A fine Scandinavian piano, a polyphone machine with discs and a pianola were all used for dancing or recitals in the ballroom. The library is the largest of any plantation house in Jamaica, with over 300 volumes, some dating back to 1697.

In 1826, Richard Barrett won £800 in a competition when the house's entryway was selected as the best mile of macadam road in Jamaica. The approach to the house must have been truly spectacular at that time, but today you must drive with a little care, as the road is in a bit of a rough condition.

Just before the town of Falmouth is **Charles Swaby's Jamaica Swamp Safari** (tel: 954-3065), home to the indigenous Jamaican crocodile and other tropical creatures. This wetland area covers about 1.6 hectares (4 acres) of mangrove swamp and has been turned into a breeding centre for crocodiles. You can take a guided walking tour of the swamp to see hatchlings, juveniles and adult crocodiles. Scenes from the James Bond film *Live and Let Die* were filmed here.

Rafting on the Martha Brae River

Falmouth

Once an important port for the shipment of molasses and sugar, **Falmouth** has many buildings dating from the early 1800s. But despite its colonial heritage, most visit Falmouth because it is the centre for rafting (daily 9am–4pm; www.jamaicarafting.com) on the **Martha Brae River**. The river is 48km (30 miles) long, and the 1½-hour raft ride covers 5km (3 miles) of navigable river that meanders through the lush countryside, where you can take in the verdant river banks and the peace and quiet. It's a cool and relaxing way to travel, almost like a tropical gondola ride. Each raft is hand-built by the raft captains to carry two adults. The rafts are made of bamboo from the surrounding countryside and can be used for only four months before they have to be replaced.

Just to the east of town is a small bay that comes to life at night. Referred to by several names (including 'Glistening Waters' and 'Luminous Lagoon'), it is officially known as

Oyster Bay (daily 7pm; www.glisteningwaters.com). Once darkness falls, the water in the bay is filled with luminescent micro-organisms that glow when agitated. You can take an evening cruise to watch this fascinating phenomenon and dip a hand in the water to make it happen yourself. The restaurant at the edge of the water is popular for a meal after the boat trip.

Cockpit Country

In the highlands and hinterlands south of Falmouth is **Cockpit Country**, an amazing and almost impenetrable landscape of limestone plateau (or 'karst') pitted with holes and fissures that have created fantastic formations. Deep depressions and high outcrops are blanketed by layers of green vegetation and topped by a lush canopy of trees, making travel difficult and at times dangerous. It is here that the Maroon people chose to live after they had been freed by their Spanish captors in 1655.

Even today there are few roads – this really is one of the last true vestiges of wilderness in Jamaica. Because much of the area is inhospitable to human activity, it is a lush area for birdlife and rare plant species that have disappeared from other parts of the island. You can find hundreds of caves in the limestone fissures, and some intrepid visitors

Duppies and Obeah

Many Jamaicans believe in the powers of magic and the underworld. Periods of bad luck or ill health are often seen as evidence of witchcraft and spells put on individuals. 'Duppies' are spirits of the dead who come back to earth. Good or evil, they can be manipulated by those still alive for mischief or revenge; 'obeah' is the local term for this type of sorcery. Look for coloured paint around the windows of homes, intended to prevent spirits from entering.

go 'spelunking', exploring their watery interiors. If you want to see the area or investigate the caves take an experienced guide and go well prepared.

Scattered Maroon villages remain, their inhabitants still making a meagre living out of the poor soil. Tours of the village of **Accompong** and the native Amerindian cave drawings nearby are organised by Cockpit Country Adventure Tours through the South Trelawny Environment Agency (tel: 610-0818; www.stea.net). One of the best times to visit is in early January, when the Maroon people hold a major festival.

The ruins at Columbus Park

Discovery Bay and Runaway Bay

Further east along the coast lies **Discovery Bay**, said to be the place where Columbus landed in 1494 on his second journey from Spain. The precise location is still disputed, as some say that he landed further along the coastline. Nevertheless, a small park on the roadside at Discovery Bay stands as a tribute to his achievement. **Columbus Park** is built on land donated by the Kaiser Bauxite Company, whose industrial site now dominates the bay. The Park includes an eclectic collection of objects from the history of Jamaica: old railway memorabilia, artefacts from sugar cane processing plants and a banana-tallying machine can all be found here.

Horses, Runaway Bay

Just outside Discovery Bay are **Green Grotto Caves** (daily 9am–4pm; charge; www.greengrottocavesja.com), which are easily accessible and safe to explore. The system stretches up to 16km (10 miles) inland and includes Green Grotto, a vast cavern with an underground lake where stalactites are clearly reflected in the glassy water, and Runaway Cave. Amerindian paintings, though fading, can still be seen on the walls of the caves. Guided tours include a boat trip on the lake.

Runaway Bay is the appropriately named area of coast-line from where the last Spanish governor fled to Cuba as the British invaders closed in. Today Runaway Bay is one of the most popular resorts on the northern coast. A series of hotel complexes has sprung up to take advantage of the fine beaches. The diving and snorkelling opportunities along the reef wall here are said to be the best in Jamaica. Most hotels offer instruction and organised dives out to **Ricky's**

Reef or the **Canyon**, two major reef areas. There are also a couple of small aircraft lying offshore (relics of drug runners who ran out of luck) that make fascinating artificial dive sites.

In the hills south of Runaway Bay is the tiny village of **Nine Mile**, where the singer Bob Marley was born and spent the early part of his life. Marley's body was brought here after his death and lies in the **Bob Marley Mausoleum** (daily 9.30am–6.30pm; charge; www.ninemilejamaica.com), where he is buried with his prized guitar. The surrounding land and the tree under which he sat as a child have been turned into a shrine to the singer, but the ambience is spoiled by the numerous 'guides' and souvenir sellers who crowd your path to the entrance. Inside the compound you'll find genuine Rastafarian guides. The whole site is painted in the bright green, red and yellow Rastafarian colours that represent nature, blood and sunshine. The mausoleum lies in a small church with other symbols of Rastafarian faith, including a photograph of Haile Selassie (their spiritual leader) and the lion of Judah depicted in a stained glass window.

St Ann's Bay

To the east is **St Ann's Bay**, birthplace of the black activist Marcus Garvey. His statue can be found on Main Street, outside the town library. St Ann's Bay is also the site of **Sevilla la Nueva** (www.jnht.com), the original Spanish settlement on Jamaica, founded in 1509, which sits just to the west of the modern town. It is one of

A detailed carving in the Bob Marley Mausoleum

the oldest populated areas on the island, where Amerindian settlements have been found dating back to AD600.

The Spanish settlers built a sugar factory here before 1526 and attempted to develop the site, but the persistent fevers contracted from mosquitoes in the swamps forced them to move and create a new capital at Spanish Town in 1538. However, Sevilla la Nueva was not completely abandoned, continuing as a working plantation and rum distillery that were later developed and expanded under British rule. The most obvious remains at the site date from this time. There are vestiges of the rum distillery, cattle pens and a large pimento barbecue for roasting allspice berries. Older remains lie scattered along the shoreline and in shallow water beyond the tidal reach. A small museum in the English great house displays finds from the site.

OCHO RIOS TO ANNOTTO BAY

Jamaica's second tourist town is a relatively recent creation. **Ocho Rios** began in the 1960s when a fishing village was developed with the aim of turning it into a resort. There are several large hotel complexes here, with more being built, and the town is also a popular destination for cruise ships.

Eight rivers

Although Ocho Rios translates as 'eight rivers' in Spanish, the name is thought to be a mistranslation of the Spanish *'las chorreras'*, meaning 'river rapids'. There are plenty of waterfalls here but not eight rivers.

Though not the prettiest town on the island, Ochi', as it is known, has beautiful natural attractions nearby and makes a good base for excursions around Jamaica, being within relatively easy reach of Kingston, the Blue Mountains *(see page 58)* and the coast road that leads to Montego Bay *(see*

Jet-skis on Turtle Beach

page 26) and Port Antonio *(see page 50)*. There is little left of old Ocho Rios: the scant remains of **Ocho Rios Fort** are probably the oldest and now lie in an industrial area, almost forgotten as the tide of progress has swept over the town.

The main waterfront area, **Turtle Beach** (charge), sits in front of the town centre. It is a wide arc of sand, shallow and sheltered. The beach is kept clean and there are facilities and refreshments available. You can hire a boat to take you snorkelling around the reef that runs all along the coast here, just a few hundred metres from the shore. Two massive all-inclusive resorts, the Sunset Jamaica Grande and the Riu Ocho Rios, overlook the beach.

Ocho Rios is a shopping mall for cruise-ship passengers. There are a number of expensive jewellery and other duty-free shops, all with goods priced in US dollars (duty-free goods must always be paid for in foreign currency). It's a veritable treasure-trove of quality gems, gold and cigars. Take a look around the incongruous pink Taj Mahal shopping mall or Soni's in the centre of town. The latter complex, with over 100 shops, probably has the widest choice. There is also a thriving craft market behind the main beach, where you will be able to haggle for locally produced goods, from a T-shirt to a necklace of semiprecious stones. Once the business day stops, there are few bars and restaurants in the town; evening activity tends to focus on the large hotels.

Dunn's River Falls

This place of fantastic natural beauty and flowing water that epitomises the Amerindian name for Jamaica, *Xaymaca* ('land of wood and water') is unfortunately a victim of its own popularity. Only 5km (3 miles) west of Ocho Rios, **Dunn's River Falls** (daily 8.30pm–4pm; charge; www.dunnsriverfallsja. com) is a series of limestone cascades surrounded by over-

Climbing Dunn's River Falls

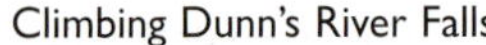

hanging vegetation that carry the water of Dunn's River almost to the sea. Lines of people, all holding hands, do a slightly wobbly 'conga' to the top, where everyone forgets decorum and gets wet in the pools. You'll be lucky if you have the pools to yourself to enjoy the kind of romantic experience advertised in the tourist brochures, as the Falls are

Fun in the falls

usually packed with tour parties and cruise ship visitors.

Guides are optional, but they are sure-footed and will take care of your camera until you reach the top. Don't forget to take a change of clothing and a towel. There are wooden walkways at the side of the Falls for those who don't want to get so wet.

Gardens, Rivers and Plantations

The road leading south from Ocho Rios climbs out of the town and twists and turns through a narrow valley of tropical vegetation called **Fern Gully**. Five km (3 miles) of giant cottonwood trees, with their tangle of thick roots, frame varieties of giant fern to create a canopy of fronds and leafy branches over the road. Insects, frogs and birds call together in a cacophony of sound. It feels so humid in the midst of the vegetation that you can imagine being on the set of a prehistoric dinosaur film. The canopy is so thick that very little light penetrates through.

Ocho Rios is surrounded by not only areas of natural beauty but also by landscaped tropical splendour. There are two fine gardens in the area, admired among gardening con-

Tubing along White River

noisseurs and each with different specialities to investigate. The first is **Coyaba River Garden and Museum** (daily 8am–5pm; charge; www.coyabagardens.com). *Coyaba* is the Arawak word for 'paradise', and this garden, set high above Ocho Rios, lives up to its name. Plants, trees and native birds are complemented by rivers, waterfalls and streams teaming with fish and turtles. The small museum at the site traces the history of the island from the time of the Amerindians.

Set on the hillside above the town, **Shaw Park Gardens** (tours daily 8am–4pm; charge; www.shawparkgardens.com) has wonderful views; it comprises 14 hectares (25 acres) of tropical plants and natural waterfalls that once formed the grounds of the Shaw Park Great House, which later became a hotel.

Twenty minutes drive from Ocho Rios, in the parish of St Mary, is **White River Valley** (daily 9am–5pm; charge; www.wrvja.com). This nature retreat offers tubing, horse riding, kayaking and hiking along forest trails and the chance to sample a sumptuous Jamaican meal. The **White River** runs east from Ocho Rios and marks the boundary between St Mary Parish and St Ann Parish. There are fresh water lagoons, rivers to swim in and picnic spots, as well as a restaurant and souvenir shop.

On the main coast road east out of Ocho Rios is **Prospect Plantation** (daily; charge; www.prospectplantationtours.com), which offers tours by jitney and horse trails through crops of coffee, bananas, plantains and sugar cane. The guides will give you plenty of information about the natural and introduced flora of the island. Visitors can also take a trip on an open carriage, ride a horse or camel, visit the butterfly house and feed ostriches.

The Spanish settled the land and grew crops here in the 17th century, but the fine Great House was built by English colonists in the 18th century. The plantation was bought in 1936 by English industrialist Sir Harold Mitchell and became an important focus for diplomatic, political and social activities in Jamaica.

Many important dignitaries have visited the house, and it has become a tradition for trees to be planted to mark each special occasion. The tour passes trees planted by the Royal family of Luxembourg, US civil rights activist and politician Andrew Young and the Duke of Edinburgh, among many others. You can plant your own tree as well. The plantation

Prospect Plantation

also houses a private academy for young people, the brain-child of Harold Mitchell. It promotes the ideal of good citizenship through hard work and community service. Many former academy students have gone on to achieve high ranks in the diplomatic and civil services.

A little further east is **Harmony Hall** (Oct–Aug Tue–Sun 10am–6pm; charge; www.harmonyhall.com), a beautiful former Methodist minister's residence built in 1886. The house, which has been home to an art gallery since 1981, has been elegantly preserved with pretty painted wood fretwork and stained shutters. The gallery on the upper floor has a collection of some of the best art and crafts in Jamaica. Original paintings from local and guest artists, ceramics and a collection of imported crafts make it a good place to find a high-quality souvenir. Beneath the gallery is an Italian restaurant. During the season there are many exhibitions and performances in the gardens of the hall.

Firefly and Annotto Bay

The coastal road continues east through the small town of **Oracabessa**, with its decaying iron fretwork, and on to **Galina Point**, the most northerly part of Jamaica. Set high on a bluff overlooking the coastline at Galina Point is **Firefly** (daily; charge), the former home of Noel Coward, dean of British theatre and cinema, and the archetypal Englishman. Coward had the house built in 1956 and lived here until his death in 1973. He is buried in the garden, at his favourite spot overlooking the sea. The house is surprisingly small and simple, with one bedroom, a tiny kitchen and a couple of social rooms.

Intuitive Art

Harmony Hall has a gallery dedicated to Intuitive Art; it includes the work of notable artists such as Allan Zion, Ras Dizzy, Deloris Anglin, Brother Brown and Beverley Oliver.

A sea view near Oracabessa

What makes it special is its position, with magnificent views of the coastline east toward Port Antonio and southeast to the peaks of the Blue Mountain range.

The parties Coward held here were legendary. Film stars such as Elizabeth Taylor, Sophia Loren and Charlie Chaplin were entertained with songs at the grand pianos that still sit in the main room. Coward valued his private life, however, and guests were never allowed to stay overnight at Firefly. They were given guest quarters at Blue Harbour on the shore, where Coward lived before building Firefly.

Nearby is the house of another famous person, an author whose fictitious protagonist has taken on an almost real persona. **Goldeneye** (www.goldeneyehotel.com) was home to Ian Fleming when he wrote all the James Bond novels. Fleming came to Jamaica in 1942 while serving in British Intelligence, decided to settle here, and bought the house in 1946. Although Bond was noted for his bravery and prowess, he was in fact named after a man of very different talents: Fleming took the name of his '007' hero from the author of the book *Birds of the West Indies*, which had been researched and written a few years earlier.

Goldeneye and its four villas are part of the Island Outpost boutique hotel chain and are available to rent. This is a popular spot for wealthy celebrities seeking a discreet but luxurious getaway. More properties are being added to the re-

Jamaica's Best Beaches

Long Bay (Negril). Seven miles of fine, golden sand gently sloping into shallow water. Low-rise development leaves room for hundreds of palm trees.

Booby Cay (Negril). Lying just off Long Bay, this tiny island provides sand all around its rocky interior.

Doctor's Cave (Montego Bay). The original tourist beach is still as popular as ever, with lots of activities. Come and be sociable.

Lime Cay (Port Royal). Just think 'Robinson Crusoe' and you'll have the right idea. But avoid it at weekends, when it's more like Grand Central Station.

Turtle Beach (Ocho Rios). Everything is in one place, and you get a great view of cruise ships arriving and departing.

Frenchman's Cove (Port Antonio). Fine white sand in sheltered coves, with lots of tropical vegetation. Wander through the coral outcrops to find a private corner.

Long Bay (eastern tip). Just the place for long romantic walks, as rolling waves break on miles of pink sand. Not suitable for swimming because of dangerous undertow.

Holland Bay (eastern tip). A stretch of fine white sand with not another soul in sight.

Treasure Beach (south coast). With numerous fishing boats, this dark volcanic sand beach is not just for tourists.

sort as part of a multimillion-dollar redevelopment.

Inland from Firefly is **Brimmer Hall Plantation** (tours Mon–Fri 9am–4pm; charge), a working plantation of 809 hectares (2,000 acres) that produces a variety of crops, including bananas, coconuts and citrus fruit. It has a beautiful, single-storey great house, made (unusually) of wood and filled with an eclectic collection of furniture from the colonies of the British

Bright flora

Empire. The tour, by jitney, shows how the plantation works, with knowledgeable staff to answer questions and give demonstrations of such skills as the correct technique for climbing coconut palms.

The main road continues to hug the north coast, but just before reaching Annotto Bay there is a turn south in the direction of Kingston. Take this route to reach **Castleton Botanical Gardens** some 18km (11 miles) inland. The 37 hectares (91 acres) of gardens are set on lands above the Wag Wag River, which twists through a steep and narrow valley. They were landscaped in 1862 with a large consignment of plants from Kew Gardens in London. Beautiful exotic plants from every corner of the British Empire were subsequently brought here before being transplanted to other gardens on the island. It might not be the oldest, but Castleton is regarded by many as the 'father' of tropical gardens in Jamaica thanks to its work in the propagation and distribution of new plant genera.

The marina at Port Antonio

PORT ANTONIO AND THE EAST

The eastern area of Jamaica is the most tropical and most beautiful part of the island. The high peaks of the Blue Mountains dominate the landscape. This is where swathes of lush rainforest mix with plantations of coffee on the high mountain slopes and meet thousands of verdant banana plants that blanket the coastal plains. The mountains attract moisture sweeping across the Atlantic Ocean and are thus often swathed in heavy rain clouds that feed the forests and fill numerous streams and rivers. There are few major roads in this area. The main route follows the coastline, circumventing the mountains and leading to some of the least-visited areas of Jamaica that are totally off the tourist track.

The western approach to Port Antonio is characterised by huge groves of banana plants, which in earlier times made the town one of the richest in the Caribbean. All along the northern coast here you will see remains of the old railway line, which once linked the plantations to the port but now mostly provides a place for children to play or animals to graze. The station houses, however, still give an impression of the grandeur of the recent past. The line was closed in 1985, but with the speed at which the native plants have reclaimed the land, it might have been 100 years ago.

Port Antonio

Port Antonio dates from 1723, when the town was called 'Titchfield' after the English estate of the Duke of Portland, who was governor of Jamaica at the time. Expansion began after the 1739 peace treaty with the Maroons, who lived inland south of the site. The area proved unsuitable for sugar cane production, but in 1871 fruit shippers began to take locally grown bananas back to Boston in the United States, and the trade was an immediate success.

In its heyday, Port Antonio was the undisputed 'banana capital of the world', with an additional benefit: the banana boats brought the first tourists to Jamaica. The wealthy visitors travelled out on the empty boat and stayed in the area after the ships took their ripening cargo back to the US or England. Fine hotels catered to the visitors' every need, and the town revelled in the money brought in from abroad.

In the town centre

Those days are long gone, as is the booming banana market: exports from South and Central America broke the Caribbean monopoly in the 1970s. However, Port

At the market

Antonio harbour still has a buzz of activity, especially in the harvesting season, as all of Jamaica's banana exports leave from here. The manual counting of the 'hands' and 'bunches' of bananas (recounted in Harry Belafonte's *Banana Boat Song*) was mechanised in the 1960s, but the work of loading the boats is still labour intensive. Developments at Port Antonio include a modern 32-slip marina, designed to blend in with the town's architecture and the West Harbour's charm. The complex has good facilities catering to vessels up to 106m (350ft). **Port Antonio Yacht Club** is the centre for sport fishing, and plays host to the International Blue Marlin Tournament every October, when the harbour is filled with sport-fishing boats from around the Caribbean.

Nestled against the Blue Mountains, the town has a beautiful setting. Two wide bays offer natural harbours, and tiny **Navy Island** sits just offshore. This was the island bought by Errol Flynn when he settled in Port Antonio in 1946; he used it as a garden extension for the large yacht he moored there. His drinking parties were legendary, and he is fondly remembered as a charming rogue. Navy Island is closed to the public but the site is slated for redevelopment.

The headland between the two main bays is called '**The Hill**'; here you will find the oldest part of town. The houses of wealthy Port Antonio residents sat away from the bustle of the busy port in a grid of seven or eight streets. This area has fallen into decay, but there are still vestiges of its fine history to be seen. Ornate ironwork now rusts, wooden fretwork moulds and paint peels, yet there remains a beauty about this aging finery. Nearby on St George's Street is **St George's Village**, an area of galleries and cafés designed as a quirky 'Amsterdam street meets Italian piazza' mall and is the brainchild of a German baroness.

For a wonderful view of the whole town, take the road up to **Bonnie View Hotel** (closed). The twin harbours, Navy Island and the Hill, can be seen from here.

The **Rio Grande**, just west of Port Antonio, is the largest river complex on Jamaica, combining a number of tributaries from the Blue Mountains. Rafts have long been a method of transport for local people, who use them to carry bananas down from the upper slopes to the port. Rafting (daily 9am–4pm; charge) on the Rio Grande was popularised by Errol Flynn and became a 'must' for tourists in the late 1940s – it is still popular today. The lush river valley cuts deep into the heart of the mountains, with sheltered habitats for birds and butterflies. A raft trip here is a more tropical experience than on the Martha Brae River *(see page 35)*. Rafters start at Berridale and complete their cruise at Rafters' Rest (St Margaret's Bay). Stop for a snack or a hike along the way.

Rafting on the Rio Grande

Frenchman's Cove

East of Port Antonio

The drive east from Port Antonio offers some of the prettiest views in Jamaica. A series of coral headlands covered in tropical vegetation reach out into the ocean. Beautiful private villas and a small number of fine resort hotels sit proudly on the headlands or nestle in the small bays. **Frenchman's Cove**, a little further east, has a beautiful sandy and shady beach, accessed through the hotel (entry charge that can include lunch on the beach). Tiny bays of soft sand sheltered by cliffs and cooling vegetation provide a completely different experience from the beaches of Montego Bay. This is the area for romantic private getaways. **San San** gained a reputation in the days of Errol Flynn for its elegant social scene; today it is an exclusive hideaway with a fine golf course. A small faded sign points the way to **Blue Lagoon**, a tiny coastal inlet with a freshwater spring just offshore. The clear fresh water mixes with the briny sea water just a few metres away and creates a hundred hues of green and blue. The freshwater hole is said to be bottomless, although the diver-explorer Jacques Cousteau dived here and measured the depth at 61m (200ft).

To the south of the coastal area, **Athenry Gardens** (formerly a plantation) has wonderful views of the surrounding mountains, but these botanical gardens are renowned much more for what is under the ground than what is above it. The **Nonsuch Caves** (daily 9am–5pm; charge) have nine chambers with dramatic formations of stalactites and stalagmites. The largest cave is called the Cathedral because of its size and scale. You'll find fossils of fish and other marine creatures that were deposited in sediment millions of years ago, when this area lay on the ocean floor. The paths are well lit and offer amazing views of the interior.

Jamaica's Eastern Tip

If you continue along the main coastal road, you'll reach **Boston Bay**. This small fishing town is the traditional centre of 'jerk', Jamaica's national dish that is now gaining a worldwide following. The jerk marinating technique was first developed by the Maroon people as a method of tenderising and cooking their pork. You will smell the roasting meat and aromatic wood fires as you arrive in the village. The fresh pork is cut into 'bellies' and scored to make it easier to cook and serve. It is then covered in the paste that gives jerk its name, placed on a rack over the pit fire and turned every few minutes until it is ready. The marinade is a good deal

Boston is best for jerk meat

spicier than you would find in a tourist restaurant, but the meat is wonderfully tender; ask for a bite-sized sample before you buy. Roasted breadfruit with the jerk provides the perfect bland antidote to the spice.

The Maroon community, descendants of proud and tenacious slaves, still live in two isolated pockets on Jamaica. **Moore Town** and **Cornwall Barracks**, hidden behind the John Crow Mountains and reached by a road from Port Antonio, make up the nucleus of the eastern group (the western Maroon area is in Cockpit Country, south of Falmouth). The settlements here were founded in 1739 after the peace treaty with the British. Maroon people are very private, still running their own affairs and paying no land taxes to the government. Although their villages don't look very different from the other rural communities on the island, it is the Maroon attitude to life which makes these societies interesting to visit. If you wish to get to know the people, you can arrange to visit them with a guide *(see page 118)*.

The coastal road makes its way around the unspoiled eastern tip of Jamaica. The long journey from the major resorts means that few visitors venture this far.

Long Bay is one of the longest and most magnificent beaches on the island, with not a hotel in sight – just nature at its best. There is no development here for two main reasons. First, this sector of coastline is most at risk from the threat of hurricanes as they whip across the Atlantic Ocean and into the Caribbean Sea. Second, the coastal swells here are extremely dangerous, preventing swimming and water sports. You'll find wooden fishing boats pulled up on the

Maroon festival

On National Heroes Day (third Monday in October) Maroons descend upon Moore Town to honour Nanny, the founder of the town and legendary 18th-century chieftainess of the Windward Maroons.

sands and nets hanging out to dry. The beach has fine pink sand; powerful breakers throw sea spray into the air. There are several beach bars that are good for lunch, and where you can sit and admire the dramatic view.

Farther south, near the fishing village of Manchioneal, are **Reach Falls** (also known as Reich Falls; Wed–Sun 8.30am–4.30pm; charge; www.reachfalls.com), perhaps the last uncommercialised falls on Jamaica. The fresh clear water comes directly down from the mountains of the John Crow National Park and falls into a deep azure pool. Scenes in the film *Cocktail* (starring Tom Cruise) were filmed in the cascades. There is a picnic area, but a restaurant is also planned for the site.

Reach Falls

On the easternmost tip of Jamaica stands the isolated **Morant Point Lighthouse**, built in 1841. With pristine mangrove swamps and the deserted sandy beaches of **Holland Bay** and **Mammee Bay**, the landscape is truly magnificent. The land stretches out for miles.

From Morant Point, the road turns west back toward Kingston. There is little to hold the attention here although the area has seen important historical events. **Port Morant**, a little way west, was the place where Captain Bligh of 'The Bounty' fame first landed breadfruit on Jamaica. The famous mutiny occurred during the first journey, when he refused the crew much-needed water, keeping it instead for the precious plants. Even after all his effort, however, only one plant survived and he had to return with a second cargo. It proved to be worth the effort for Bligh, who received a reward of 1,500 guineas.

Morant Bay is the major settlement in southeast Jamaica; it played a big part in one of the turning points in the history of the island. The Morant Bay rebellion of 1865 was led by Paul Bogle and supported by George William Gordon (after whom Gordon House, the Jamaican seat of Government, is named). The uprising and the violent reaction of the British forces resulted in the destruction of many of the historic buildings in the town, which never really recovered. The most interesting attraction is a statue that commemorates Bogle, located outside the tiny courthouse. This strong, powerful depiction was designed and sculpted by Edna Manley.

The Blue Mountains

Covering much of the interior of the eastern part of the island are the magnificent **Blue Mountains**, the highest on Jamaica. There are five major peaks ranging from John Crow Mountain at 1,753m (5,750ft) to Blue Mountain Peak at 2,256m (7,402ft). The mountains are blanketed with thick, verdant forests watered by regular tropical downpours from the heavy clouds that surround the high peaks. The blue heat haze that surrounds the mountains and gives them their name can best be seen on warm afternoons, when it is possible to see peak after peak stretching into the distance.

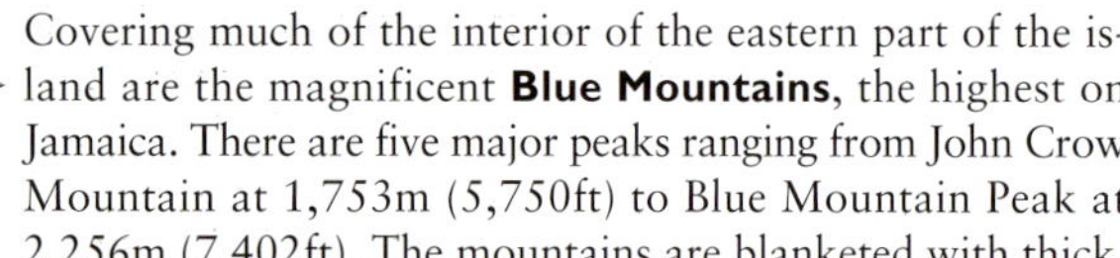

Bogle

A statue of Paul Bogle stands in front of the court house in Morant Bay; it is a reconstruction of the one burnt down during the 1865 rebellion. Bogle and his brother were hanged from the centre arch of the gutted building.

View over the Blue Mountains

A number of slopes and valleys have remained untouched by man and offer a habitat for rare flora and fauna including the national bird, the streamertail hummingbird (commonly called the doctor bird), and the giant swallowtail butterfly *(Papilio homerus)*, the second largest in the world. The richness of the environment around the Blue Mountains has long been recognised; the **Blue and John Crow Mountains National Park** was established in 1993 to manage and protect 78,200 hectares (193,200 acres) of land being damaged by illegal loggers and slash and burn farmers.

The best way to view the Blue Mountains is to drive from Buff Bay on the north coast down to Kingston on the B1 highway, although the road can be impassable after heavy rain due to landslides. Always check road conditions before you depart. The interior of the mountain range and the most beautiful parts of the parks are not accessible to vehicles: the best way to experience them is to take a guided walk. There are a variety of routes, which can last from a morning to several days. The hike to **Blue Mountain Peak** itself is not for the inexperienced and will take a full day; if you want to see the sunrise, start out at 2am to reach the summit in time to greet another Jamaican day *(see page 118)*. Whichever option you choose, remember to take some warm clothing, because temperatures here are a few degrees lower than on the coast, even on a sunny day. When the clouds come in, it can feel quite chilly.

In addition to their tropical splendour, the Blue Mountains have slopes at an altitude above 3,000m (9,840ft), which are perfect for growing coffee. Blue Mountain coffee is said by aficionados to be the best in the world. The **coffee plantations** lie in the humid heights, where soil conditions and the slow growing process (five years from germination to harvesting) produce a fine crop with a high yield. This natural affinity between the Blue Mountains and the coffee bean is amazing, because the first plants are said to have arrived in Jamaica by accident.

In 1723 Louis XV of France ordered three *arabica* coffee plants to be sent from Yemen to the French island of Martinique, which lies farther south. Two plants died on the long journey and the third mysteriously found its way to Jamaica. This plant was the start of the Jamaican coffee industry, the most important business in this part of the island for more than 250 years. Because of the topography and the delicate nature of the plants, much of the work is still done by hand and traditional working practices have endured.

Mountain coffee

Coffee beans normally take four months to develop from blossom to harvest, but in the Blue Mountains where the weather is cool, damp and cloudy, they take 10 months, resulting in a harder, larger bean. The sugars in the bean caramelise on roasting, giving the unique flavour.

Downtown Kingston

KINGSTON AND ENVIRONS

With one of the largest natural harbours in the world – lying between lush green hills and the Caribbean Sea – Kingston Bay became the perfect site for one of the biggest ports in the Caribbean. Commercial success made **Kingston** the capital of Jamaica in 1872.

Now home to more than a quarter of the population of Jamaica, it is a huge city. Modern 'New Kingston', with its office buildings and high rise blocks, is the administrative heart of Jamaica, with government offices, consulates and boutiques. To the northeast lie the foothills of the Blue Mountain range, where wealthy Kingstonians build houses to take advantage of the cooling breezes. The poor live on the flat, dusty plains below, where country life has simply been transplanted to the city. Goats wander the streets and people live in tiny tin shacks with few amenities. They sit up against several other shacks that make up blocks of properties (or 'yards'). The violence and crime that have been a feature of life in Kingston over the years, centre on political and gang rivalries within these yards.

Downtown

Downtown Kingston, once a model of British colonial 'pomp and circumstance', is now surrounded by some of the poorest and most densely populated neighbourhoods in the city. It is not a place to wander around at night. However, during the day the area is full of office workers going about their business and petty crime is no worse than in any other capital city. Take normal precautions.

The city centre developed around the waterfront. Fruit, rum and spices were once transported from the old docks; today the harbour area has been transformed. In 1982, the **Jamaica Conference Centre** was built; there are also

Jamaica's 'Higglers'

You'll meet these persuasive salespeople all over Jamaica, at craft markets or on the beaches. Their goal is to sell you the souvenir that you can't leave Jamaica without. However, since there are no set prices, you must engage in the intricate game of 'haggling' if you want to buy and not get ripped off.

Don't engage in haggling if you are really not interested in buying an article. It only creates bad feelings, and you may feel the sharp edge of a 'patois' tongue. A firm but honest 'No' is better than five minutes of negotiation followed by no sale. Higglers view this as disrespect for them on your part.

As a guideline, aim to start your negotiation at about half the initial price offered. Sale price should generally be about 20 percent lower than the vendor's original offer.

galleries and historical collections that celebrate the culture of the island. The **National Gallery** (Tue–Thur 10am–4.30pm, Fri 10am–4pm, Sat 10am–3pm; charge; www.galleryjamaica.com), at 12 Ocean Boulevard, has a comprehensive collection of Jamaican paintings, sculpture and other art, including works from the 1920s; there are many works by Edna

Exhibit at the National Gallery

Manley (1900–87), one of Jamaica's foremost modern artists, wife of Norman Manley and mother of Michael Manley, both former Prime Ministers. Beside the docks is **Victoria Craft Market**, the domain of the famous 'higglers', the assertive women who run the small stalls. The building, constructed in 1872, is a fine example of Victorian colonial architecture.

Away from the waterfront, the streets in the city centre feature a number of historic buildings. On Duke Street you will find **Headquarters House**, built in 1755. The house was selected as the seat of the island legislature in 1872, when the capital was moved from Spanish Town to Kingston. It is now the base of Jamaica National Heritage Trust. Nearby **Gordon House**, built in 1960, is home to today's legislators; it was named after George William Gordon, leader of the Morant Bay rebellion, who became a member of the Jamaica Assembly and spoke out for the rights of the poor and oppressed.

National Heroes Park, at the north end of Duke Street, used to be a racetrack (you can still make out the shape of the circuit). All of Jamaica's national heroes are buried

Wall of pride

here with impressive monuments symbolising their lives and achievements: Sir Norman Manley and his artist wife, Edna, Sir Alexander Bustamante, Paul Bogle, George William Gordon, Sam Sharpe, Marcus Garvey and Nanny of the Maroons, while the north section is reserved for the burial of former prime ministers and other individuals who have contributed to the political, social and educational development of the country.

The **Institute of Jamaica**, on East Street, was founded in 1879 to encourage research in science, art and literature in the true spirit of the Victorian age. It also houses the **Natural History Museum** (Mon–Thur 8.30am–5pm, Fri 8.30am–4pm; charge; www.instituteofjamaica.org.jm), on Tower Street, the oldest museum on the island, with a collection of over 125,000 types of preserved plant species. The **National Library** next door to the Institute has the largest collection of books, articles and papers on the history of the West Indies and is an important archive.

King Street is the heart of the city centre and the main shopping street. Here is **William Grant Park**, originally Victoria Park, in reality a small town square that was opened in 1879 with a life-sized statue of Queen Victoria at its centre. In 1977, it was renamed after the black nationalist leader. The **Parade**, the streets surrounding the park, once heard the marching steps of British soldiers; it was here that slaves were beaten or hanged as punishment for their 'crimes'. Now it is a hive of 'higgler' activity and the hub for bus routes around the city.

New Kingston

New Kingston is the modern commercial centre of the Corporate Area (parishes of Kingston and St Andrew), and is the hub of business, with hotels, fast food places and night spots. Near the Jamaica Pegasus hotel is **Emancipation Park**, popular with the lunch crowd in the day and joggers in the evening.

On the edge of the district is **Devon House** (gardens daily 9.30am–10pm, shops Mon–Sat 10am–6pm, restaurants until 10pm; www.devonhousejamaica.com), built in 1881 as a plantation house for George Steibel, the first black millionaire of Jamaica. The beautiful exterior is complemented by the fine period furniture housed inside. The mansion was renovated in 1967, 1982 and again in 2008. The gardens are a cool place to sit, and the stables and outbuildings have been converted into a lovely courtyard containing attractive shops, cafés, an ice cream parlour and a notable restaurant. Some shops and eating places are open on Sunday.

Nearby on Hope Road are **Jamaica House**, containing the offices of the Prime Minister; **Vale Royal**, the Prime Minister's official residence; and **King's House**, home of the Governor General, originally the residence of the Bishop of Jamaica. None of these grand buildings is open to the public.

Devon House

Marley memorabilia

Tuff Gong Recording Studios used to be located at 56 Hope Road, a small compound where reggae musician, Bob Marley, lived and worked. Since his death it has been transformed into the **Bob Marley Museum** (guided tours Mon–Sat 9.30am–4pm; charge; www.bobmarley-foundation.com/museum) and managed by the Marley family to protect the memory of his life. The museum has some interesting displays, including Marley's gold records and photographs of activity at the studios. Some of his personal effects can be found in the modest bedroom where he slept.

Port Royal

A spit of land reaches out south of the city across Kingston Bay, sheltering the famous harbour. Called the **Palisadoes** (after the Spanish word *palisade*, meaning 'defence'), this is an arid area of magnificent cacti and margins of mangrove that shelter populations of seabirds. Halfway along the narrow peninsula you'll find **Norman Manley International Airport**, the main airport of entry for Kingston and the eastern part of the island. At the tip of the Palisadoes is Port Royal.

When the British arrived in the late 1650s they built Fort Cromwell here; it was renamed **Fort Charles** following the restoration of the British monarchy in 1662. **Port Royal**, the town surrounding the fort, earned a reputation as the most raucous and debauched city in the Caribbean. With the help of the pirates who made the town their base, Port Royal became a rich city, with the income from sugar and rum combined with stolen Spanish treasure *(see pages 15–6)*. After the 1692 earthquake that devastated the city and buried much of its wealth, Port Royal never fully recovered. Some treasures have been salvaged (along with everyday articles such as pewter cutlery and plates); much still lies only a few feet below the waves.

Kingston replaced Port Royal as the commercial centre of the island. However, Fort Charles was rebuilt as a military and naval garrison, and it protected Jamaica and much of the English Caribbean for 250 years until yet another earthquake struck in 1907. The brick fort, home to Lord Horatio Nelson during 1779, still stands proud and 'ship-shape'. The large cannons on the battlements now guard **Fort Charles Maritime Museum** (Mon–Thur 10am–5pm, Fri 10am–4pm; charge; www.jnht.com), which documents the maritime history of Jamaica. Here you can view models

View from Port Royal

both of the fort and of the types of ships that sailed the Caribbean over the centuries.

Landslides and small quakes have taken their toll on sites at the Fort, and **Giddy House** is a perfect example of this. The small, square building once stored ordnance, but it has been left at a very precarious angle, sinking back into the sand. The sadly dilapidated **Old Naval Hospital** can be found a little farther to the north; its distinctive iron supports were brought to Jamaica in 1819 and were designed to be both earthquake and hurricane proof. The hospital building now houses the **National Archaeological and Historical Museum**, which displays a fascinating collection of finds from the sunken city of Port Royal.

Residents of the little village of Port Royal make their living from fishing. On weekends, it is popular with families from Kingston who come to enjoy the fresh air or a fried fish dinner at one of the little restaurants that spill out on to the streets. From the marina you can take a boat to **Lime Cay**, which lies just to the south of Port Royal. This tiny 'desert island' offers the chance to sunbathe on sandy shores or snorkel in clear water and feel a million miles away from Kingston.

Jamaica's Predatory Pest

If you travel around the island, you are bound to catch sight of a mongoose running across the road into the undergrowth. This small furry creature was introduced to Jamaica during colonial times to prey on snakes and rats, which were a danger both to the people and to the crops. The mongoose was extremely successful in ridding the island of these two problems. However, it then began to look for other things to eat. It is now considered to be the most populous and vicious pest on the island, preying on domestic chickens as well as eating the eggs and chicks of native wild birds.

The south coast is peaceful and relatively undeveloped

CENTRAL HIGHLANDS AND THE SOUTH

Away from the large towns and tourist resorts, life continues in time-honoured tradition. In central and south Jamaica, numerous small settlements and family farms dot the countryside, where you'll see donkeys tethered at the roadside or trotting along the lanes carrying large baskets. A network of smaller roads that knit the villages together make travelling a real adventure: there are few signposts (and even fewer people) to point the way if you do become lost.

The contrast between the landscape of the central highlands and the south coast could not be more marked. The highlands are cool, with verdant hills rolling through the heart of Jamaica. As you travel south, the landscape changes. Acres of grassland surround coral limestone columns and escarpments. Low-growing acacia trees replace tropical vegetation, with the landscape characterised much

Fresh tropical fruit on display at the market

more by prairie than by palm trees. The southernmost margins of the island – away from the pressure of human development – are a haven for wildlife.

Spanish Town

The Spanish settlers in 16th-century Jamaica, having tired of the disease-ridden Sevilla la Nueva in the north, looked for a new site for their capital city. They chose the flatlands around the Rio Cobre and, in 1534, established Villa de la Vega, later called St Jago de la Vega. The British captured Jamaica in 1655 and henceforth gave the settlement the rather unimaginative name 'Spanish Town'. As capital of a wealthy colony, **Spanish Town** had its fair share of fine buildings that included courthouses, administrative offices and official residences. However, the capital was moved in 1872 to Kingston, the commercial heart of Jamaica, and a malaise enveloped Spanish Town from which it never recovered.

The elegant Georgian buildings along the **Parade**, have fallen into disrepair. The most striking building in the Parade is the white stone edifice that houses the **Rodney Memorial**, constructed at great expense in gratitude after Admiral Rodney's fleet saved Jamaica by defeating the French at the Battle of Les Saintes in 1782. One wing houses the **Jamaica Archives and Records Office**, which preserves original documents from throughout the island's history.

On the west side of the square is **Old King's House** (built in 1762), which was the official residence of the British governor; it was here that the proclamation of emancipation was issued in 1838. It was a fine building was destroyed by fire in 1925. Only the façade is original; the building behind it is modern. The **Jamaican People's Museum of Craft and Technology** (Mon–Thur 9.30am–4.30pm, Fri until 3.30pm; charge), housed in a reconstructed corner of the house, features a model of how the building looked before the fire. The other two sides of this fine Georgian square are taken up by the ruins of the old Court House and what was the House of Assembly, now local government offices.

The **Taino Museum** (Mon–Thur 8.30am–4.30pm, Fri 9.30am–3.30pm; charge), 3km (2 miles) east of Spanish Town, comprises the most important collection of Amerindian artefacts in Jamaica. The museum re-creates the lifestyle of Amerindians in a series of models illustrating how their villages and daily activities might have looked.

The **Hellshire Hills**, south of Spanish Town, come as a surprise to those who think that the tropics can only be lush and green. The landscape here is underscored by limestone and receives fewer than 760mm (30in) of rain per year. There is little soil to support plants, resulting in a desert-like landscape of cactus and low scrub trees. The area has become the last haven for many of the native

Hellshire

but almost extinct plants, animals and birds of Jamaica. Here you'll find the last few Jamaican iguanas and yellow snakes. The string of beaches along the coast are popular destinations for Kingstonians on weekends.

Mandeville

Mandeville sits to the west of Spanish Town in the Don Figuero Mountains. Its cool air and pretty setting made it a favourite retreat for colonial families right up to the end of British rule in Jamaica in 1962. They came to spend their weekends here, away from the hot and humid atmosphere of Kingston. Today, it is a favourite place for wealthy Jamaican families for very much the same reason. The town was laid out in 1816 and named after Lord Mandeville, the eldest son of the Duke of Manchester, after whom Manchester Parish was named. The English modelled the town and its buildings on those of their homeland, and one can imagine the village greens, tennis and golf clubs, and grassy verges taken from a typical London suburb.

There are a number of interesting attractions lying to the west of Mandeville. **Appleton Distillery** (Mon–Sat 9am–4pm; charge; www.appletonrum.com) is situated in rolling hills just to the south of Cockpit Country. Sugar cane was brought to Jamaica by the Spanish in the early 16th century. Much of the crop was exported, but it was treated before being shipped and a by-product of the treatment was molasses, used as a basis for making rum. Many major sugar factories had a distillery on site, usually producing alcohol for local consumption. Appleton Distillery, in operation since 1749, pro-

Cool Manchester

Manchester's cool climate (20°C/70°F in the summer and 16°C/60°F in the winter) appeals to Jamaicans returning to the island after decades living abroad in the UK and North America.

Having a swinging time a YS Falls

duces 42,000 litres (74,000 pints) of rum every day. Much of this is 'overproof' rum, the basis of intoxicating rum punches, but the finest rum is aged in casks for up to 30 years to produce a spirit comparable to brandy or cognac. The distillery offers a tour of the rum plant and the opportunity to taste and buy a range of rum and rum-based drinks.

In some parts of the island, bamboo was planted along the roadside to provide shelter for people travelling in the heat of the day. The groves of bamboo also created places where slaves would congregate without being seen by their masters. Much of the bamboo has since decayed or been dug up, but **Bamboo Avenue**, the one remaining section, can be found on the main A2 road between Mandeville and Black River. It is a 3-km (2-mile) tunnel of bamboo surrounded by sugar cane, with somnolent grazing cattle tethered along its length.

Nearby are **YS Falls** (Tue–Sun 9.30am–3.30pm; charge; www.ysfalls.com), found on a working thoroughbred horse

Take a tour down Black River

stud and cattle ranch that dates from 1684. The water cascades 50m (164ft) over seven tiered falls and has formed two large pools and a small cave system at the base of the second drop.

When Tropical Storm Lily ripped through here in September 2002 the top fall collapsed, leaving it less impressive than before. It is not possible to walk up through the water as at Dunn's River, but steps have been erected at the side to take you to a platform at the foot of the first cascade. You can swim in the pools at each level and a rope swing has been created at the middle level.

The falls are surrounded by mature native forests and vibrant tropical flowers, but an area of grassy lawn has been created for sunbathing and picnicking. There are changing rooms and a small refreshment area. It is said that the falls got their name from the initials of the two original landowners, John Yates and Colonel Richard Scott. The cattle and sugar barrels exported from the plantation had these initials branded onto them.

Black River

Once a major port on the south coast, **Black River** is now a small, sleepy town on the banks of the river from which it took its name. Its industry was the export of red logwood and the dyes of indigo and Prussian blue, which were extremely valuable in Britain. There is still some fine Georgian architecture here, but most visitors come to see the **Great Morass Mangrove Swamp**. This area, which should not be confused with the Great Morass near Negril, is about 6,500 hectares (16,000 acres) of freshwater and tidal wetlands. The Mangrove Swamp and rush beds are an important habitat for many species of birds and fish, as well as home to a small population of Jamaican crocodiles. Smaller than the Florida species and said to be more docile, they grow to 6m (20ft) in length and can live to an age of 100 years.

The Black River, at 71km (44 miles), is the longest in Jamaica; it was an arterial route used to transport rum and lumber from the inland plantations. It still provides a living for many families, either from fishing or from the harvesting of bullrushes for basket making. Tours on the river and into the Great Morass start from Black River town *(see page 74)*. The route takes you into the **Man-grove Alley**, said to be the quietest place in Jamaica, where you can search out the basking reptiles and native birds that call this place home. Roots, which look like cathedral organ pipes, drop from the higher trees. Your guide will turn off the engine and an eerie silence will envelop the boat. Choose a tour company according to your interests; some guides concentrate on seeing crocodiles while others give a more rounded wildlife tour.

A Black River man takes a break

The pool at Jake's,
Treasure Beach

Treasure Beach

The southern coastline of Jamaica has so far resisted the pressure from big developers, partly because it has few main roads. Those who do venture here are rewarded with beautiful scenery and friendly people. **Treasure Beach** is the only resort area to speak of, with just a handful of hotels stretching across three sandy bays. There are also cottages for rent, which make this an ideal spot for walkers and visitors who prefer a quiet getaway to the busy all-inclusive resorts on the north coast.

The local population of St Elizabeth Parish still makes a living from fishing and their wooden boats rest high on the dark, volcanic sand. You'll be able to spend the day relaxing without being hassled. If you want to buy a souvenir, just hail the mobile shop that drives slowly along the road looking for customers. There's very little to do here but chill out.

East of Treasure Beach are some beautiful strips of coast. On one is the Little Ochi seafood restaurant, a simple affair on the beach in the fishing village of **Alligator Pond**. The government-owned **Alligator Hole** (also known as Canoe Valley Wetland) on the eastern side of Long Bay has been awarded official status for protection of the last remaining manatee population on Jamaica. This pristine region of freshwater and saltwater swamps, edged with limestone cliffs, offers a refuge to this gentle creature as well as to birds and land crabs.

NEGRIL AND THE WEST

This area, the furthest from Kingston, lagged behind other parts of Jamaica in modern development, protected from the commercial activity of the east by the limestone landscape of Cockpit Country, making travel and communication difficult. It was an outpost of pirate activity in the 17th and 18th centuries. Today, Negril is at the forefront of the tourist industry.

Heading west from Montego Bay, the main road hugs the coastline. Just a little way out of town is **Tryall Estate**. This old pineapple plantation had fallen into decline before being transformed into the first (and some say the best) resort hotel on the island. The manicured greens of the golf course can be seen on both sides of the main coast road, along with the plantation's water wheel, which still turns with the weight of river water. A number of golf tournaments are held here every year.

On the beach in Negril

Negril

A pirate hideaway in the 1600s, **Negril** was rediscovered in the 1960s by the 'children of love' and others looking for an alternative lifestyle. It is now popular with 'spring breakers', US students seeking a party and a good time. Jamaicans say that Negril isn't a place – it's 'a state of mind' where almost anything goes. There are few hippies left today, but the pleasures are still pretty earthy: it's not unusual to see topless sunbathers or catch a faint whiff of 'aromatic' smoke. You're also more likely to see true Rastafarians here, along with others who simply enjoy living the image of the religion without abiding by its strict rules. Dreadlocks and tams (colourful knitted hats) are everywhere, along with the passing salutations. Located on the western tip of Jamaica, Negril is also one of the best places in the world for watching the sun go down.

To the east is Long Bay, a vast expanse of fantastic sandy beach, while to the west is West End, with coral cliffs that drop directly into the clear blue ocean.

Long Bay is 11km (7 miles) of sublime fine sand, gentle azure water and cooling palm trees. It is one of the best beaches in the Caribbean, parts of which are public. Several large resort hotels have been built here but there are also small and intimate, family-run hotels if you want a more personal touch.

Aloe Vera

As you lie on the beach, you are sure to be offered an aloe vera massage by a passing 'higgler'. You will be told that it will help you develop a golden tan, but be aware that aloe – although an excellent treatment for sunburn – should not be used as a tanning or sun-protection product. Make sure that you use a product with a suitably high SPF (Sunscreen Protection Factor) to protect your skin while you sunbathe.

Vendors and hair braiders can be found in pink booths along the beach, but any number of 'unofficial' ladies who braid can be found at the cafés and bars. There are endless rows of small craft stalls under the palm trees, but the craft market at the town end of Long Bay has everything in one place.

Across Norman Manley Boulevard from the beach is **Kool Runnings Water Park** (daily; charge; www.kool runnings.com), an adventure park with action-packed attractions for all the family, including water slides of all shapes and sizes. At the northern end is the **Anancy Village** for dry land activities such as go-karting, a bungee trampoline, carousel rides, restaurants and bars.

Catching a wave

At the top of Long Bay is **Booby Cay**, a small island just a short distance offshore. The tree-topped rock surrounded by golden sandy beaches is the archetypal 'desert island' – a great place for snorkelling, sunbathing, or picnics. You can rent a canoe to get there under your own steam or take a leisurely ride in one of the many small ferry boats departing from Long Bay.

The coral cliffs of **West End** provide a total contrast to Long Bay. Diving and snorkelling are the things to do here among the rocks and caves, and the shimmering waters house some wonderful sea life. West End is also the place to

Cliff jumping at Rick's Cafe

take in the sunset. Almost everyone heads to **Rick's Café**, perched on the cliff top, to have a drink and set up the camera. While you're waiting, you'll be entertained by the divers who launch themselves from the tops of tiny perches into the azure sea some 9m (30ft) below. They are often joined by courageous tourists, who usually get more applause than the professionals.

Alternatively, a sunset cruise on a catamaran will transport you effortlessly to West End, and you can lie offshore away from the crowds with your rum punch. The cliff road ends at the Victorian-era **Old Lighthouse**, which still protects ships passing this rocky promontory.

To the east of Negril is the **Great Morass**, a wetland area covering around 2,400 hectares (5,900 acres). The wetland and the **Royal Palm Reserve** (daily 9am–6pm; charge; www. royalpalmreserve.com) are managed by the Negril Area Environmental Protection Trust (NEPT), which preserves one of the largest swathes of Royal Palm – Jamaica's national plant – left on the island. Numbers have dwindled due to the rapid tourist development, but the palms here are now protected. The wetlands support a large number of birds and land crabs. Birdwatching, nature walks, fishing and horse riding tours can be arranged. There have been attempts to drain the wetlands, but this damaged not only the Great Morass but also areas of the coral reef offshore. Both are now officially protected.

To the South

The road along the coastline to the south travels through busy agricultural towns and fishing villages mostly untouched by tourism. The first settlement is **Little London**, which has a relatively large Indian population that provides the markets with much of Jamaica's fresh produce. Next is **Savanna-la-Mar**, the bustling capital of Westmoreland Parish, where **Mannings School** (built in 1738) retains its original, brightly coloured, colonial-style wooden buildings, beautifully preserved – a perfect environment for the children in their smart uniforms. Nearby at Ferris Cross is **Paradise Park**, a working cattle ranch where many scenes from the film *Papillon* (starring Steve McQueen and Dustin Hoffman) were shot.

South of Savanna-la-Mar the road hugs the coast, here narrow beaches brim with faded wooden *pirogue* canoes and other boats. This is one of Jamaica's prime fishing areas, and around **Bluefields** you'll see local men carrying their catch home. The speciality of this region is spicy shrimp, caught and cooked within minutes at stalls along the roadside. Local women offer bags of this snack for a few dollars, but try one first before you buy – they can be very hot and spicy. Beyond here, at Whitehouse, is the all-inclusive Sandals Whitehouse Resort, the only large tourist development on the south coast.

WHAT TO DO

Jamaica cannot claim to have the very best beaches, reefs, or sport fishing in the Caribbean. However, it is indeed one of the best 'all-around' islands in the region, offering a wide range of opportunities for a variety of activities. Under the warm island sun you can enjoy water sports or you can just relax on the sand doing nothing at all. Nightlife includes an abundance of reggae music and dancing, and if you're here at the right time of year you can attend some of the world's biggest music festivals. For those in shopping mode, the choices are many: woodcarvings, colourful clothing, coffee and (of course) rum.

SPORTS AND OUTDOOR ACTIVITIES

Beaches and Water Sports

Spending the day on the beach taking in the sun is one of the primary reasons tourists visit Jamaica. Every resort area has its own famous beaches with their own particular beauty. Many of the beaches are private, meaning that you must pay admission, but they are well maintained and offer lots of facilities. Negril has the great expanse of Long Bay and the small 'desert island' of Booby Cay, while Montego Bay has the shorter expanses of Doctor's Cave Beach and Cornwall Beach. In Ocho Rios you will find Turtle Beach, where you can watch the cruise boats docking at the pontoon in the bay. Port Antonio beaches are now the domains of the fine hotels on San San Bay, Frenchman's Cove and Dragon Bay, all of which are tiny coves protected by rocky tropical outcrops. Long Bay on the eastern coast is wonderful be-

Jewellery on sale at a beach shop, Runaway Beach

Snorkelling in Negril

cause it is remote and un-crowded, but it is not suit-able for swimming because of strong currents. Treasure Beach on the south coast has dark volcanic sand beaches that are home to colourful fishing boats.

At the major resorts, beaches are kept clean and facilities for a range of water sports are readily available. Jet skiing is popular in the sheltered waters near the beaches. If you are adventurous, you can go parasailing, with a boat pulling you along above the beach and waterfront. This is particularly exciting along Long Bay at Negril. A couple of bars have even installed large trampolines offshore, where you can swim out and bounce above the water.

If you do intend to take part in any sporting activity, make sure to check that your travel insurance policy spe-cifically covers it. Some policies have clauses that exclude certain sports.

Snorkelling

Jamaica is particularly good for snorkelling, with many reefs and rocky promontories to explore very close to the shore. There are also a number of shallow areas between reefs that offer a fascinating view of various types of sea life. Beauti-ful tropical fish in iridescent blues and greens search through the coral for food, and in deeper waters you can spot big-ger fish such as rays and nurse sharks. All the major resorts have small boats offering trips to offshore sites if you want to snorkel in deeper water.

The West End at Negril is ideal for snorkelling. The coral cliffs drop down into a clear azure sea, and there are hundreds of caves and canyons to explore. Montego Bay has the Marine Park with a range of environments. At Doctor's Cave Beach you can snorkel in an area where warm spring water meets the sea, or join a guide to go further out to the Coyoba, Seaworld or Royal reefs where the fish are larger and more varied. Further east, Runaway Bay has fine reefs running parallel to the line of hotels along the beach. Ocho Rios has a wonderful shallow reef running east from Turtle Beach for safe snorkelling.

Diving

Much of the northern coast of Jamaica is fringed by areas of deep reef wall that make diving a pleasure. Although some sections of reef have been damaged in recent years, there are

Jamaica's Top Dive Sites

Negril. Pete Wreck is an old submerged tug boat. Throne Room is a huge cavern with yellow sponges. Sharks' Reef is home to nurse sharks, while you can see eels at Rock Cliff Reef.

Montego Bay. The Marine Park contains underwater walls of coral. Airport Reef and Widowmaker's Cave are two of the most famous sites.

Runaway Bay. Ricky's Reef at a depth of 30m (90ft) is covered in gorgonians and lettuce coral, while at Pockets Reef there are sunken light aircraft that crashed and are now being colonised by sea creatures.

Ocho Rios. The reef wall drops over 900m (nearly 3,000ft) but comes close to shore, offering nearby dives with a variety of fish and other aquatic life. A deliberately-sunk former minesweeper is now home to a range of marine life.

Kingston. To dive the sunken city of Port Royal you must obtain special permission. For information contact a local dive operator.

still many areas with a wide range of fish and other marine creatures to see. Most of the major resort areas offer diving opportunities and certified training facilities for those who want to learn how to dive. Your hotel may offer certified instruction or guided dives. For more information contact the Jamaica Tourist Board *(see page 125)* for a selection of approved and certified dive operators.

Boat Charters, River Tours and Rafting

If you don't want to get into the water but you'd still like to see aquatic life on the reef, then take a glass-bottomed boat trip. There are a number of companies in all the major resorts. At Negril and Ocho Rios, the boats tie up along the main beach; you can negotiate a price while you sunbathe. The boats in Montego Bay all dock at the same place, so you can compare prices and facilities. Pier 1 has a range of options, from small boats to large submersible craft that will take you under the water in complete comfort; why not try a trip with MoBay Undersea Tours (tel: 940-4465; www.mobayunderseatours. com). If you are not a confident swimmer, a boat is probably the best way to enter this very different aquatic world.

Take a trip on a glass bottom boat from Buccaneer Bay

Visitors can explore Jamaica's inland waters by raft on the Martha Brae River *(see page 35)* or Rio Grande *(see page 53)*. Take a trip down the Black River to experience the 'Great Morass' *(see page 74;* for tours contact Irie Safari, tel: 634-4232) and see crocodiles in action, or you can simply get wet and picnic at YS Falls *(see page 73*; tel: 634-2454), near Mandeville.

Crocodile smile at Black River

Sport Fishing

Sport fishing is also a popular activity. Port Antonio hosts a major international angling tournament each October. Blue-and-white marlin are the prized catch: the waters around Jamaica are especially rich in these magnificent fish and this is the oldest marlin-fishing tournament in the Caribbean. Other fish are plentiful: you only have to see what the local fishermen are bringing in. You will find sport-fishing boats for hire at the marinas in the major resorts: Bay Pointe at Montego Bay, the main beach in Ocho Rios, Morgan's Harbour Hotel at Port Royal in Kingston and Errol Flynn Marina at Port Antonio. You can hire a boat with equipment and crew by the day or half day.

Other Activities

Golf

Jamaica has an excellent range of golf courses, from small nine-hole to championship 18-hole courses. Several important tournaments take place on the island during the year, where

Golf at Sandals, Ocho Rios

you can watch international players from the PGA and the LPGA compete.

Montego Bay has fine courses, professionally designed and maintained in peak condition. The most famous course is at the Tryall resort, west of Montego Bay, where the greens caress the undulating coastal slopes. To the east of Montego Bay, where the coastal plain is flat and wide and an ideal landscape for golf, there are several large hotels that have courses. The four best are the Half Moon Golf Club, the White Witch course at Ritz Carlton Rose Hall, the Cinnamon Hill course at Wyndham Rose Hall Country Club and Super-Clubs Golf Club (formerly Ironshore), all created by internationally acclaimed designers and offering a challenge for all ability levels. These courses are open to the public.

Walking, Hiking and Cycling

Jamaica is a perfect island for walking, hiking or mountain biking, with a range of different environments from coastline to tropical peaks and from dry limestone landscapes to lush river valleys. More and more visitors are looking to get off the beaten track, at least for part of their holiday.

A guide is recommended for a trek to the Blue Mountain Peak or a hike into the Cockpit Country. Several companies organise tours that can be tailored to your needs. The Southern Trelawny Environmental Association (STEA) provides local guides for Cockpit Country tours (tel: 610-0818; www.stea.nct). Valley Hikes (tel: 993-3881) and Grand Valley Tours (tel: 993-4116; www.portantoniojamaica.com/gvt.html), based in Port Antonio, have a variety of hikes in the picturesque Rio Grande Valley and northern sections of the Blue and John Crow mountains. Sun Venture Tours run hiking, caving, safari, sightseeing and adventure tours island-wide (tel: 960-6685; www.sunventuretours.com). They also organise cycling tours in the mountains behind Kingston. For mountain biking on footpaths and goat trails, Rusty's X-cellent Adventures (tel: 957-0155; http://rusty.nyws.com/services.htm) in Negril arrange guided tours designed for all levels of fitness. *(See also Bicycle Rental, pages 108–9).*

For news and information about competitive cycling meets, charity rides and racing, contact the Jamaica Cycling Federation (www.jamaicacycling.com). The annual Bikeathon Jamaica Challenge is held in April: the route stretches from Montego Bay along the north coast to Lucea and back, with distances ranging from 5km (3 miles) for children up to 75km (47 miles) for professional cyclists.

Horse Riding

There are several places in Jamaica to get in the saddle. Try the facilities at the Half Moon Hotel (tel: 953-2286) or the stables on the Barnett Estate (tel: 952-2382).

Colourful flora

Cricket on the green

Spectator Sports

Spectator sports tend to be seasonal. Depending on the time of year, you can attend a range of competitive events.

Cricket

There are few things more genteel on a hot afternoon than watching a match unfold and hearing the sound of leather striking willow. The professional season in Jamaica runs from January to August each year and international matches are usually played at Sabina Park, Kingston, upgraded for the Cricket World Cup in 2007 (the opening ceremony was held at the multi-purpose stadium at Greenfields, Trelawny, east of Falmouth). You might also come across a local game in almost any village. The English introduced cricket to the island, but Jamaican players and spectators bow to nobody in their obvious enthusiasm for the game.

Polo

Matches are played at several places but you can watch an international match at Kingston Polo Club (tel: 968-9493), St Ann Polo Club, Drax Hall (tel: 972-2762) and at Chukka Cove (tel: 972-2506) near St Ann's Bay in the north. Major tournaments take place November to February and August.

Horse Racing

There is a track at Caymanas Park near Kingston. Betting is in Jamaican dollars only.

NIGHTLIFE AND ENTERTAINMENT

Jamaicans love to listen (and dance) to local music, of which there is a vast range. Reggae, with its bouncy 'backbeat', has been a huge influence on pop music throughout the world. Jamaica has one of the world's most intense grassroots music traditions with a competitive, lucrative recording industry.

You'll find live music in bars and restaurants every night. These will be advertised in the free tourist magazines in your hotel, or out on the street booming from speakers on tops of cars. Negril, Ocho Rios and Montego Bay all have nightclubs that stay open very late. *What's On Jamaica* (www.whatsonjamaica.com) has an excellent weekly entertainment guide.

Many hotels have Jamaican nights where you can watch a dance show and do some dancing yourself. These traditional evenings often feature the rhythms of the wider Caribbean, such as calypso (Trinidad) and *merengue* (Dominican Republic).

The island's biggest music festival is 'Reggae Sumfest' (www.reggaesumfest.com), which is held at a variety of venues in Montego Bay each July/August and features local and international artists. Ocho Rios also has an annual jazz festival.

Having a ball in Margaritaville, Montego Bay

Local art on sale

SHOPPING

One thing that you notice about Jamaica is that many shops come to you. You won't be able to walk down the street without someone approaching you with crafts and other commodities. Buying from the street traders means there is no set price, and some people feel uncomfortable about haggling. Follow the advice on *page 62* to increase your confidence and remember two things: bargaining is supposed to be an enjoyable interaction, and nobody can make you buy something that you don't want.

The major resort towns all have duty-free shopping centres with a range of jewellery, perfume, leather goods and other quality products from around the world. Some of these items can be purchased with savings of up to 30 percent on prices back home, but not everything offers such good value.

Arts and Crafts

Wood carving. The Jamaican people are highly skilled in the art of carving wood. It is one aspect of communal pride that has carried on since colonial times. Woodcarvings are a major souvenir product, and there is a huge range from fine carved pieces to objects in the rough 'naive' style. Rastafarian faces and figures are a popular choice, as are such African animals as giraffe and elephants.

You will see natural wood and also a range of colourful productions in the red, yellow and green Rasta colours. The wide range of styles is matched by an equally wide range of quality, so do check the pieces carefully before you buy. Different types of wood have different weights and different finishes. Some of the pieces are extremely lightweight, but the dark *lignum vitae* wood is heavy and has a beautiful finish when carved.

Don't buy articles if the wood still looks green: it has not been allowed to season properly and will split as it dries.

Jewellery. There is also an amazing range of jewellery made from local products and semiprecious stones. These are extremely pretty and inexpensive, but you should be aware that some of the materials used are from protected species.

Both tortoiseshell and coral are still on sale. Don't buy them. Not only is it illegal to import these articles back into your home country, but it encourages traders to take more of these endangered living creatures from the sea. Some traders will tell you that the coral jewellery or tortoiseshell they are selling was not taken from the sea but was washed up on the beaches; this is just a sales ploy.

Basket weaving. You will also find a wide variety of basketware made locally from the rushes that can be found in huge beds all around the island. The dried-rush baskets are still used in many households today, and they make a very practical souvenir of your visit to Jamaica.

Art and ceramics. If you want to spend a bit more money on handcrafted goods, there are a number of galleries around the island where you can buy paintings and ceramics by some of the leading artists in Jamaica and the wider Caribbean. Harmony Hall at Ocho Rios is one, and the Half Moon Shopping Centre (just east of Montego Bay) also has a gallery. If you find yourself in Port Antonio, St George Village has a number of studios featuring works of modern artists. To see crafts being made, tour the Wassi Art Pottery Factory (tel: 974-5044; www.wassiart.com), near Ocho Rios. There is also a variety of beautiful and unusual pottery on display and for sale at the studio and pottery works.

Blue Mountain coffee

Clothing

Cool clothing remains a popular choice for shoppers, and Jamaica offers a wide range from designer wear in the boutiques of Kingston to the practical batik sarongs and T-shirts sold in beach stalls. If you travel light, you can buy your holiday wardrobe when you reach the island.

Coffee

Blue Mountain coffee can be bought and taken home in a number of forms. The roasted beans are sold in small sacks or in vacuum-packed foil containers. The beans can also be ground and then packed in tins or foil packs. Presentation packs (pretty printed bags) add an attractive exterior to the delicious contents. You can buy direct from the growers after a farm tour and a tasting. Worth a visit is the Old Tavern Coffee Estate (tel: 924-2785; www.oldtaverncoffee.com) run by the Twyman family in Green Hills, Portland, where an informative

Jamaican rum packs a punch

tour is provided. Remember that High Mountain coffee is not of the same quality as Blue Mountain coffee.

Rum

The drink that sustained a thousand pirates and generations of local people, Jamaican rum is said to be the best in the Caribbean – although other islands may beg to differ. Try before you buy. Appleton Distillery (tel: 963-9215) in St Elizabeth offers a free tasting session as part of its tour, including some mixed-rum drinks that are less alcoholic but equally delicious *(see page 104)*. All these products are available throughout the island and at duty-free shops in the airport.

Cigars

For over 40 years, Jamaica has had a small-scale industry that produces a range of well-regarded cigars. These can be bought duty-free to take home with you. However, Cuban cigars are also a major business here. Jamaica is only 145km (90 miles) from the south coast of Cuba and imports a full range of what are reputed to be the finest cigars in the world, though they cannot be brought legally back to the USA.

CHILDREN'S JAMAICA

Jamaica is an ideal island for children of all ages. Kids can play for hours at the beach building sandcastles, swimming, or simply splashing in the water. Long Bay at Negril is perfect for young children, but all the major resorts have clean, safe beaches with good facilities. Older children will enjoy snorkelling, scuba diving or taking a ride on a glass-bottomed boat. Take a trip underwater in a submersible boat at Montego Bay and your kids will be captivated by the sea life that lies so close to the shore.

Adventurous kids will enjoy a cruise up Black River into the **Great Morass Mangrove Swamp** to meet crocodiles, which come so close you can almost shake hands with them. At **Dunn's River Falls** there's excitement for children and adults alike, plus lots of water activities. For a more relaxing kind of fun try floating down the **Martha Brae River** on a raft. The rafts take one child under 12 with two adults; older children must travel on a separate raft.

Most large hotel complexes have children's clubs where kids can spend the whole day enjoying activities and excursions. Conversely, some hotels on Jamaica operate on an 'adults-only' policy.

Remember to cover every inch of young skin with a high factor sun cream, limit kids' time in the sun for the first few days of your holiday and always keep them out of the midday sun. Also make sure that they are well supervised whenever they are near the water.

Negril is perfect for children

Festivals and Events

Exact dates vary. If you want to attend a particular event, check with the Jamaica Tourist Board *(see page 124)* or check www.whatsonjamaica.com.

January *Rebel Salute Music Festival; Air Jamaica Jazz & Blues Festival* (Montego Bay).

6 January *Accompong Maroon Festival.*

February *Pineapple Cup Yacht Race (*Miami to Montego Bay*); Reggae Summerfest (*Ocho Rios*); Fi Wi Sinting (*African heritage festival, Portland*).*

6 February *Bob Marley Birthday Bash.*

March *West End Reggae Festival* (Negril); *Fun in the Son (Gospel Festival* in Ocho Rios).

April *Jamaica Carnival* (around Easter, Kingston); *Montego Bay Yacht Club Easter Regatta.*

May *Calabash International Literary Festival* (Jake's, Treasure Beach).

June *Ocho Rios Jazz Festival; Kingston on the Edge Art Festival.*

July *International Reggae Day Festival* (Kingston); *Portland Jerk Festival; Reggae Sumfest* (international music festival, Montego Bay); *Little Ochi Seafood Festival* (Alligator Pond, Mandeville).

August *Port Royal Music Festival* (Kingston); *Mello Go Roun'* (festival of performing arts, Kingston); *Jamaica Push Cart Derby* (Ocho Rios); *Seville Emancipation Jubilee* (heritage festival, Ocho Rios).

6 August *Independence Day Parade* (street carnival featuring *junkanoo* dancers, Kingston/island wide).

September *Negril Sprint Triathlon* (Long Bay); *Jamaica Spice Food Festival* (Ocho Rios).

October *Nyammins and Jammins Festival* (Montego Bay); *Jamaica Open* (golf tournament, Half Moon Golf Club, Montego Bay); *Port Antonio International Marlin Tournament (see page 87)* and *Port Antonio Local Canoe Tournament; National Heroes Day* (island wide).

December *Reggae Marathon and Half Marathon* (Negril); *Jonkunnu* (also known as Junkanoo; street parades and Christmas celebrations across the island); *JMMC All Stages Rally Jamaica* (motorsports race, Kingston).

EATING OUT

Jamaica is a large and fertile island. Fruits and vegetables grow in abundance on family farms, and the land is grazed by cattle, goats and pigs. The clear waters are full of edible fish as well as lobster, shrimp and other seafood. You will be offered an amazing variety of dishes, all very fresh. The range of eating opportunities across the island is remarkable, from cheap street stalls and beach bars to fine restaurants offering international and 'new Jamaican' cooking.

What to Eat

The island's historical and ethnic heritage has contributed to a unique cuisine: it is a story of African cooking techniques and Indian spices meeting Caribbean ingredients. Jamaican food has a reputation for being spicy but, surprisingly, most of the dishes are tasty but not hot. The heat comes from a sauce found in a little bottle that is always on the table, allowing you to add as much spice as you like – or none at all. This hot sauce is manufactured on the island with a secret recipe based on 'Scotch bonnet' pepper, one of the hottest in the world. A little goes a long way, so start carefully and discover your personal taste level.

You will find tame versions of all Jamaican dishes on the menu at large hotels, which often provide a night of Jamaican cuisine where you can sample a range of dishes along with some Jamaican entertainment.

Jamaican Cuisine

Ackee and saltfish. This dish was once a staple food for the enslaved Africans who were transported to the island, and it is now the official national dish of Jamaica. *Ackee*, which is native to Ghana in West Africa, is a vegetable now found in great abundance on Jamaica. The ackee is harvested only when it is ripe, as it is poisonous otherwise. It is chopped and cooked until it takes on the appearance of firm scrambled eggs. The enslaved Africans added a small amount of protein-rich salted codfish for a cheap and nutritious way to start the day. Today ackee is often served with other types of fish or with bacon as part of a traditional Jamaican breakfast. It comes with various kinds of carbohydrate such as dumplings called 'Johnny cakes', or perhaps with *bammy*, a cassava pancake.

Meat dishes. Jamaicans always cook their meat well rather than rare, so you won't have to worry about the dangers of undercooked meat. But meat served in local restaurants is chopped into pieces with a cleaver rather than being butchered and trimmed, so beware of sharp pieces of bone which might be present in the prepared dish.

Ackee, fresh from the tree

Jerk. The modern national dish of Jamaica is 'jerk', which takes its name from the hot marinade used to season meats or fish. You will find it everywhere from the menus of fine restaurants to beach bars and street barbecue stalls. The dish was invented in Maroon country (near Boston Bay in the east of the island) and was originally used to tenderise pork, which was then cooked slowly and served hot and tender. The marinade became popular across the island for all meat, and today you can eat jerk chicken and even jerk fish. The Boston recipe is a mixture of 21 spices and very piquant indeed.

You can watch jerk pork and chicken being prepared in Boston Bay and then try it for yourself. The meat is freshly butchered (the animals are slaughtered in the mornings under the auspices of health inspectors), then marinated and cooked within hours. You will be served the meat with breadfruit, which has a neutral flavour to cool the palate. In other parts of the island, the jerk ranges in flavour and hotness. In hotels and international restaurants, it can be quite mild; you'll find that Jamaicans snub their noses at such offerings.

Goat curry. There are herds of goats alongside all the highways and byways of Jamaica. Goat curry (referred to as 'curry goat') became part of the Jamaican diet following the arrival of the Indian itinerant workers who came to work the plantations following the abolition of slavery. The curry style has adapted over the generations and is now really more of a flavour than a true Indian method of preparation.

Fish dishes. A most amazing array of fish and shellfish can be found in the waters surrounding Jamaica. You can be guaranteed absolutely fresh seafood because the small boats come in daily with their catch. In many restaurants the 'catch of the day' will be the tastiest and freshest option. It might be tuna, snapper, or kingfish; whatever the choice, it will always be superb. The lobster and conch are also fresh and delicious, although they are seasonal. Different areas of the island specialise in certain types of seafood. Around Bluefields,

Full of flavour

Authentic Jamaican cuisine is flavoursome thanks to the spices and seasonings used to marinate the meat and fish, usually overnight. They can include pimento, allspice, thyme, garlic, cloves, ginger and fiery scotch bonnet (peppers).

Jerk chicken with rice and peas

south of Negril, it is spicy shrimp, and at Middle Quarter you will find Escovitch fish, which is fried and then pickled.

Rice and peas. Most main dishes are accompanied by a side dish of rice and peas. It originated as an inexpensive and nutritious option in colonial times, when it could be served as a meal in itself when money was scarce. The 'peas' (actually red or kidney beans) and the rice are cooked slowly together with a bit of coconut milk.

Vegetables and fruit. Because fresh vegetables in Jamaica are varied and plentiful, you will always be given a generous accompaniment with any main dish. The list includes *callaloo* (a spinach-like vegetable), yam, breadfruit, pumpkin and potatoes. Starchy vegetables have been a staple of Jamaican diets since the days of slavery when they were needed to provide energy for hard labour.

You can sample the abundant fresh fruits from stalls in the street or from hawkers on the beach. Hotels will have a won-

Fresh fruit and vegetables in Spanish Town

derful selection at breakfast or to finish a meal in the evening. Bananas are obviously popular, but you can also choose from guava, mango, papaya, pineapple and coconut. There is in addition a range of unusual fruits found only in Jamaica. Look out for sweetsop and soursop (rough-skinned fruits, said to be aphrodisiacs and best made into a milky drink) along with the star apple and the *ugli* (a citrus fruit).

As one of the island's major crops, the banana has a special place in Jamaican cuisine. It is eaten raw but also in many hot desserts. You can have banana fritters and, for a touch of luxury, bananas flambéed in Jamaican rum.

Other hot and cold desserts include tarts and custard, which is traditionally flavoured with coconut cream. Ice creams made with fresh fruit are also extremely refreshing: 'matrimony' is a Jamaican favourite, which mixes orange and star apples with cream. Other local favourites include rum and raisin and grapenut ice cream.

Snacks. Jamaican fast food consists of a number of cheap dishes that are prepared at home or bought at roadside stalls for lunch on the run. 'Patties' are thin oven-baked pastries filled with meat, fish or vegetables. 'Stamp-and-go' are fish fritters, so called because just before being cooked they are flattened with the palm of the hand. These dishes are often served as hors d'oeuvres in hotels or in private homes.

International Cuisine

In addition to serving toned-down versions of local dishes, Jamaica's resorts offer a wide range of international cuisine. There are a number of Italian restaurants all across the island, from those offering quick trattoria-style service to up-scale dining establishments with full service. Visitors seeking Mexican and Chinese cooking will find choices as well, and the comforts of American and Continental food are also available. There are branches of international fast-food chains in Kingston, Montego Bay and Ocho Rios if you want a burger or fried chicken.

What to Drink

One advantage of a trip to Jamaica is that you can drink the tap water. You can be assured that food washed in tap water is safe to eat and that ice made from it is safe in your sodas or frozen daiquiris.

Beer. Red Stripe, a lager-type beer, has long been associated with Jamaica. It is light and very refreshing on a long, hot Jamaican day. You will find it in every café and bar. However, Jamaicans also have a liking for stout

Red Stripe

You might hear some older locals asking for a 'policeman' at the bar. Don't be alarmed – they just want a Red Stripe beer. The name was taken from the stripes on the trousers and cap of the Jamaican police uniform.

Appleton rum

beers, which they like to drink at room temperature. You will find that Dragon Stout and Guinness are widely available. You can order your drink cold if you don't mind the locals having a little joke at your expense.

Rum. The first thing that you will be offered when you arrive at your hotel is a rum cocktail. Appleton, the 'overproof' white rum, is the best-known brand, used as the basis for almost limitless recipes. Whichever rum you choose, be careful because they all 'pack a punch'. Many hotels and bars will have their own special recipes, but most will combine rum with fresh fruit juice, lime, or coconut milk. Rum can also be combined with cream and other flavourings to produce a range of smooth after-dinner drinks. Perhaps the best known liqueur is Tia Maria (produced from the Jamaican coffee bean), which makes the perfect accompaniment to a hot cup of coffee.

Non-alcoholic drinks. The choice of fruit juices is huge, and you can find single juices or blends in every bar and restaurant. 'Ting', a refreshing fizzy grapefruit drink, is locally produced. Jamaica also produces a ginger ale which has a little more kick than the standard and is extremely refreshing in the heat of the day. You will find all the internationally recognised brands of fizzy drinks readily available.

Cocoa. Jamaican cocoa beans *(see picture on page 105)* contain a chemical which is a mild stimulant. The roasted and ground beans or seeds can be used to make a delicious hot drink as well as chocolate.

Jamaican coffee. Said to be the best in the world and extremely expensive due to the small crop and high demand, most Blue Mountain coffee is exported, so you might not find it in every establishment on the island. The coffee is extremely mild and low in caffeine, with a hint of natural sweetness.

During the 1960s, the reputation of Blue Mountain coffee suffered because inferior lowland beans began to be blended with quality mountain beans to increase the crop and meet demand. In 1973, the government stepped in to create an official standard for Blue Mountain coffee, thus restoring confidence in the marketplace. Today, only coffee grown at an altitude of 610m (2,000ft) or above can be sold as 100 percent Blue Mountain. You might also discover products advertised as 'blended' Blue Mountain coffee; these will contain at least 20 percent Blue Mountain beans.

A cocoa pod contains seeds that make delicious chocolate

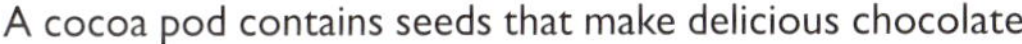

HANDY TRAVEL TIPS

An A–Z Summary of Practical Information

A

ACCOMMODATION

Jamaica has a full range of accommodation, from basic beach shacks to luxury all-inclusive hotels, and small family-run hotels can be found dotted among massive chain resorts. There are a number of options for room and meal plans, including bed and breakfast, half board, full board and all-inclusive, or you can opt for room only.

In Kingston the best hotels are designed for business travellers, while guest houses are of variable quality and not particularly cheap.

All-inclusive resorts were invented in Jamaica and are found mostly along the north and west coasts. Some hotels accept couples only and others cater for families, but most offer a wide range of sporting activities, wedding and honeymoon packages and excursions. Although all-inclusive hotels offer all facilities for one price, it is important to check the quality offered in each resort, as these do vary.

There are also some boutique hotels where you can be pampered in luxury and enjoy some of the island's most beautiful scenery on the coast and in the mountains. These do not come cheap. Many of the small luxury hotels have been around since the 1950s, attracting movie stars and the glitterati before mass tourism arrived. Recent additions to this sector include the Island Outpost group.

Jamaica also has a wide range of private villas for rent, with or without staff. Contact the Jamaican Association of Villas and Apartments (JAVA), Pineapple Place, Ocho Rios (tel: 974-2508, www.villasinjamaica.com) for more details.

For general information on rental of cabins in the Blue Mountains, contact the Jamaica Conservation and Development Trust, the local NGO responsible for the management of the Blue and John Crow Mountains National Park (tel: 920-8278/9, www.green jamaica.org.jm).

Prices change dramatically between high and low season. Low season is from mid-April to mid-December, and you can make savings of up to 40 percent during this period. High season is extremely busy, so it is important to make reservations well in advance to guarantee the accommodation of your choice.

AIRPORTS (see also GETTING THERE)

There are two international airports on the island: Norman Manley International Airport at Kingston and Sangster International Airport at Montego Bay. Manley serves Kingston and the east of the island; it also caters to international business travellers. Sangster International serves the north coast, the west of the island and also handles the charter aircraft that fly to the island.

A trip from Norman Manley Airport to Kingston takes 20 minutes and is 15km (9½ miles). There is a bus service, but a taxi direct to your destination is a more sensible option. Transfer time to Port Antonio is around three hours.

Central Montego Bay is only 5 minutes from Sangster International Airport, and there are taxis outside the terminal building even though many hotels and resorts will provide transport for the short transfer. Transfers to other resorts by coach are as follows: Ocho Rios is around 2 hours, Runaway Bay 1½ hours and Negril 1 hour. An ongoing highway construction programme is set to improve journey times.

There are also a number of domestic airports: Negril Aerodrome, Boscobel (near Ocho Rios), Ken Jones Airport (Port Antonio) and Tinson Pen (Kingston), which operate transfer flights from the two international airports. In Kingston, most domestic flights leave from Tinson Pen.

B

BICYCLE RENTAL

Bicycle rental is a sensible way to see a little more of the area where you are based. It is particularly useful in Negril, where the land is flat. It is also possible to undertake bicycle tours into the Blue Mountains and around Port Antonio, along the relatively quiet roads. Contact Blue Mountain Bicycle Tours, 121 Main Street in Ocho Rios (tel: 974-7075, www.bmtoursja.com) or, in Negril, Dependable Bike Rental (tel: 957-4764). Cycles can be rented by the day or by the week.

BUDGETING FOR YOUR TRIP

To help you budget for your trip, here are some prices for the things you will need.

Flights to Jamaica. A charter flight from London in the UK to Montego Bay can cost as little as £230 including taxes, while a scheduled flight to either Kingston or Montego Bay starts from around £400. From the US, the best deals are from Miami, Florida, with return tickets on budget airlines starting from about US$130 excluding tax.

Accommodation. A room can range in price from US$40 in low season for a hideaway such as Ital Rest Cottages *(see page 133)* to US$1,800 per night for a suite in a top-class hotel such as the Jamaica Inn *(see page 129)* in high season, depending on whether you opt for room only (EP) or for a fully inclusive luxury resort hotel (AI). For a room in a less expensive hotel, allow US$40–$70 per person; for a medium-standard hotel, prices range from US$100–$180 per night. All-inclusive resorts and luxury hotels start at over US$200 per day but can rise to more then US$350, depending on the facilities and comfort level provided.

Self catering. Rental rates of houses, cottages and studios in resorts start from US$500 per week, but for a villa with fully fitted kitchen and maid service expect to pay over US$1,500 per week, and for the very luxurious (such as those at Blue Lagoon), from US$6,500 per week. These prices can prove to be good value on a per-person basis.

Meals. For lunch in a moderately priced but good establishment allow US$20 per person plus drinks; for dinner, allow US$40 per person plus drinks. Street stalls and beach shacks offer the best value food, such as patties (pasties).

Car rental. Allow around US$40–$125 per day depending on the size of car. The lower figure is the price for a compact car in low season, while the higher price is for a 4x4. If you want to hire a car with a driver, expect to pay around US$250 for a 10-hour day, including fuel.

Local transport. Bus fares are cheap, both in town and for longer distances, if you have the stomach for a journey at speed, often on twisting mountain roads. In Kingston the urban bus fare is US$0.60. However, travelling by bus is not recommended for the fainthearted. Taxis charge about US$5 for a short journey but check the fare beforehand. For long journeys the taxi fare could be more than hiring a car, but you can negotiate a deal with a small taxi company.

Leaving the island. A departure tax of J$1,000, or the equivalent in foreign currency, is payable at the airport unless included in the price of your ticket.

C

CAMPING

Camping is not a recommended form of accommodation in Jamaica.

CAR RENTAL

Jamaica is the third-largest of the Caribbean islands, and to see all its delights it is best to hire private transport. The condition of the roads and Jamaican driving habits do create concerns for car renters (see DRIVING), but with common sense and care, renting a car should enhance your trip, not spoil it.

The major car rental companies have offices at the two international airports:

Hertz: Kingston (tel: 924-8028), Montego Bay (tel: 979-0438, at the airport). Head office can be reached at 952-4250 or 952-5200.

Avis: Kingston (tel: 926-1560), Montego Bay (tel: 952-2362).

Island Car Rentals is the largest local fleet: Kingston (tel: 926-8861), Montego Bay (tel: 952-5771), Ocho Rios (tel: 974-2666).

Local companies are more competitively priced than the international companies and provide a similar quality of service. Always satisfy yourself as to the age and condition of the car before confirming the booking. You can specify whether you want a manual or automatic transmission. Many companies make an extra charge for delivering the car to your hotel; this can amount to another day's rental charge.

All national driving licences will be recognised by rental companies. Drivers must have held a licence for at least one year before they can rent. All renters must give a deposit, which ranges from US$500 to US$1,000; if you are under 25 years of age, there will also be a bond to comply with insurance regulations. A credit card is the most sensible method of giving the deposit, although cash can also be used.

In the US, some insurance companies cover hire cars; check to see whether you are covered on your policy or through your credit card before purchasing insurance. Damage waiver is recommended, which will add around US$15 per day to your costs.

In high season it is important to book a car in advance, as demand will be high. In low season you should be able to negotiate a package that will give you a better price, and it can often be better to wait rather than book in advance.

Service stations are open daily and accept cash only (Jamaican dollars or US dollars) for fuel.

CLIMATE

Jamaica is a tropical island. It has virtually no change in seasons, the temperature varying between 25°C and 28°C (77°F and 83°F), although it is cooler in the mountains. Rainfall averages around 198cm (78in) each year and is greatest between August and November, which is considered low season for visitors. However, rain can fall in short, heavy tropical showers at all times of the year, especially in the afternoon. Rainfall varies considerably between the wetter east and the drier west of the island. Hurricane season, which afflicts the whole Caribbean, runs from the beginning of June through to the end of November.

Average daily temperatures for Jamaica:

	J	F	M	A	M	J	J	A	S	O	N	D
°C	25	25	25	26	27	28	28	28	28	27	26	25
°F	77	77	77	79	81	83	83	83	83	81	79	77

CLOTHING

Lightweight clothing is sensible throughout the year along the coasts. Many people manage happily with T-shirts and shorts during the day, and wear something a little more formal in the evening. Cotton or other breathable materials are ideal. In the mountains, sweaters are a good idea for evenings or in case of a change in the weather. If you plan to visit interior towns or Kingston, more conservative clothing might be appropriate. Beachwear is acceptable only in the immediate area of the beach and not in shops and banks.

A hat and sunglasses are important, as the sun is very strong, especially in the middle of the day. When you first arrive, always make sure that you have clothing to cover your skin to prevent burning; a lightweight long-sleeved shirt is fine.

Footwear should be light and comfortable: a pair of sandals or flip-flops for the beach, along with a smarter choice for evenings. If you plan to visit the Blue Mountains, a pair of stout shoes or walking boots is essential.

CRIME AND SAFETY

Jamaica, and Kingston in particular, have a reputation for crime and violence, but in fact there are few attacks on tourists and the Jamaican countryside has a comparatively low crime rate. Much of the violent crime is confined to about four police districts in Kingston, which are prone to drug gangs and political inter-neighbourhood rivalry. As with any city, visitors are advised to exercise caution.

The use of marijuana, or 'ganja' (as it is known on the island), is not uncommon among Jamaicans of all classes; many smoke it, while others use it as a medicinal herb. Rastafarians use it as a sacrament in religious observances. The drug is easily available and most visitors will be offered a supply at some stage during their holiday. Jamaican law is very clear: it is strictly illegal to possess or use marijuana, and punishments are severe for those who are caught.

For other forms of crime, simply take the same precautions you would observe in any other destination. Do not wear expensive jewellery or leave your possessions lying around in public places. Do not carry large amounts of cash. Take travellers' cheques or credit cards instead of cash; these offer more protection because you can obtain replacements if they are stolen. Always leave things that you don't need locked in your room safety deposit box, and keep all valuables in the hotel safe. Don't walk into unlit areas after dark and don't get into a car with someone that you don't know.

The Jamaican authorities have increased security patrols in the resort areas, and you will see the blue uniforms of the 'Tourist Police' on the beaches. Many hotels also employ private security personnel, who patrol beaches and hotel entrances to deter hawkers and others.

Many Jamaican men make a living as impromptu (and definitely unofficial) guides, and they might approach you in the street or on the beach. Use caution in your dealings and use accredited companies only. Do not accept offers to ride in unauthorised taxis (official taxis have red number plates); they will not be insured to carry fare-paying passengers.

Always take out a travel insurance policy and photocopy important documents in case you need to make a claim.

CUSTOMS AND ENTRY REQUIREMENTS

Residents of the US and most Commonwealth and European countries do not need a visa to visit Jamaica, but must carry a passport valid for at least six months and a return ticket. Visitors from Canada can enter with a valid passport, naturalisation certificate, or photo ID with birth certificate, but a passport is essential to transit the US.

No vaccinations are required unless you have visited the following areas within six weeks before your visit to Jamaica: Asia, Africa, Central and South America, Dominican Republic, Haiti and Trinidad and Tobago. Please contact the Jamaica Tourist Board *(see page 124)* for further advice if you have travelled to these destinations.

Items that may be brought into Jamaica duty-free are 1 quart of liquor (except rum) and 1 pound of tobacco in any form. Restricted items include certain types of fresh goods (flowers, plants, honey, fruits, vegetables) and coffee. Strictly prohibited are firearms, explosives and dangerous drugs. Kosher foods may be brought into Jamaica but require special documentation.

You should declare any unusual or expensive items (such as cameras or electrical goods) on arrival to assure the authorities that they are for personal use only.

D

DRIVING

Driving in Jamaica can be an adventure or a worry. The roads are in very bad condition and there is a lot of traffic. You might find cars driving towards you on the wrong side of the road, only to realise that they are avoiding a large pothole on their own side of the street. Always drive with utmost care and be ready to stop at any moment for potholes, animals and people. Cross-country routes, particularly in the area of the Blue Mountains, are prone to flooding or landslides. After periods of rain, you should always check before setting out to be sure that the road is passable; ask bus or truck drivers or employees at your hotel.

There is a big road-building programme at the moment, so expect roadworks and delays. The North Coastal Highway is being built in stages: Negril–Montego Bay and Falmouth–Ocho Rios are complete; and the Ocho Rios–Port Antonio section is due to be finished by the end of 2008. Highway 2000 in the south will connect Kingston with Montego Bay via St Catherine, Manchester, St Elizabeth, Westmoreland and Hanover, and Kingston with Ocho Rios via St Ann.

Speed limits and safety. Vehicles drive on the left, and speed limits are 50km/h (30mph) in towns and 80km/h (50mph) in rural areas. Despite this, many Jamaican drivers ignore the speed limits and drive at a dangerous speed. Always drive at a safe pace and allow plenty of time to reach your destination. Roundabouts (or traffic circles) are common. Give way to any traffic from the right at roundabouts.

Road signs feature easily recognisable international symbols. However, you will find that distance signs can be in either miles or kilometres, which can create confusion. The unit of measurement used will always be indicated at the side of the number. The area around Treasure Beach (in the south) is not well signposted, so patience and good map-reading skills will be useful there.

Many Jamaicans do not own vehicles, so offering lifts to neighbours is normal. Pedestrians might raise a hand for a lift as you pass, especially in country areas. Many vehicles will stop suddenly or will not signal before they pull off the road to pick up passengers. When driving in Jamaica, you should not pick up passengers.

Fuel and service. There are fuel stations open seven days a week in all towns. Always carry out basic checks on a rental vehicle when you take delivery of it and before setting out. Public telephones are rare in the interior; if you do break down, it could be hours before you get help, unless you have a mobile phone. If you have mechanical difficulties, contact your rental company for assistance.

Parking. When parking in towns or near beaches, try to find a car park with some security, and always park with the car in full view. At night, always park in a well-lit location. Never leave anything of value in your car, and put all other items out of sight in the boot.

E

ELECTRICITY

Jamaica operates at 110 volts/50 cycles as standard; current at 220 volts is available in some hotels on the island. Appliances with US and Canadian plugs can be used without adapters, but appliances from the UK and Europe will require one.

EMBASSIES AND CONSULATES

All diplomatic representatives have offices in Kingston.

Canada: 3 West Kings House Road, Waterloo Road Entrance, Kingston 10, tel: 926-1500, www.jamaica.gc.ca.

France: 13 Hillcrest Avenue, Kingston 6, tel: 978-0210, www.amba france-jm-bm.org.

Germany: 10 Waterloo Road, Kingston 10, tel: 926-6728, www.kingston.diplo.de.

UK: 28 Trafalgar Road, Kingston 10, tel: 510-0700, www.british highcommission.gov.uk/jamaica.

US: 142 Old Hope Rd, 3rd floor, Kingston 6, tel: 702-6000, http://kingston.usembassy.gov.

EMERGENCIES

In the event of an emergency, call **911** for police and **110** for fire or ambulance services.

G

GAY AND LESBIAN TRAVELLERS

Homosexuality is an offence, punishable by prison in Jamaica. Consequently, homophobia is rife and there is no open gay scene.

GETTING THERE (see also AIRPORTS)

By air. Flying into Jamaica is an easy option from the US, Canada and Europe. Miami, New York, Atlanta, Chicago and Toronto are all major hubs in North America, with easy connections to other US and Canadian cities. London is the hub for Europe, with easy connections for the UK and Ireland.

The following major airlines fly into Jamaica: Air Jamaica, Air Canada, American Airlines, British Airways, Northwest Airlines, US Air and Virgin Atlantic. Scheduled flights will normally land at Norman Manley International Airport in Kingston. If you will be spending most of your time around Montego Bay or Negril, it would be much more convenient to land at Sangster International Airport at Montego Bay, where the transfer time is much shorter.

Many other scheduled airlines and charter companies offer services depending on the time of year, with more services during high season. Most charter flights land at Montego Bay in the north. Consult a travel agent for the most appropriate service for your holiday plans.

Visitors from Australia and New Zealand can travel through either the US or Britain to pick up a connection to Jamaica. Both directions involve long journeys and possibly a stopover en route, so consult an airline specialist for advice about schedules and costs.

By sea. Many tourists visit Jamaica as a port-of-call on a cruise. Montego Bay and Ocho Rios are major cruise destinations, with comprehensive facilities for cruise passengers. Both ports are well placed to offer tours to a range of attractions that can be visited on your day ashore. Cruise companies all offer different packages with different prices; individual ships belonging to the same company have different facilities and levels of comfort and luxury. Before booking, research what is available on board as thoroughly as you would a hotel on land to ensure you get the trip that you want.

GUIDES AND TOURS

There is a comprehensive tour programme offering visits to sites across the island. These can be booked either through your own tour or cruise company or through the Tourist Board offices. For those who don't want to hire a car, this is an ideal way to see more of Jamaica. Tour companies will pick you up at your hotel and bring you back at the end of the day. Full-day tours often include lunch.

JUTA (Jamaican Union of Travellers Association) provides licensed taxis and tour buses for excursions to all major attractions (tel: 968-7088); there are JUTA branches around the island. JUTA can also arrange individual itineraries. Prices for the same tour do vary, and you can save money by booking directly with JUTA or with the Jamaica Tourist Board, rather than through your own tour operator.

H

HEALTH AND MEDICAL CARE

For medical emergencies, phone **110**.

Hygiene standards are generally high in Jámaica, and the tap water is drinkable. There are some minor nuisances that can be avoided. Mosquitoes can be a problem, especially just after sunset, so cover up or apply insect repellent. Don't step on the spiny sea urchins as you snorkel or dive; the spines will embed themselves in your flesh and the sores can become infected. Go easy on the alcohol, especially in the sunshine, as this can lead to dehydration. Take time to build a tan to avoid sunburn and sunstroke; use a sunscreen with a sufficiently high SPF. If you are already taking medication, it would be sensible to anticipate your needs for the trip, as pharmacies here are less well stocked than at home.

Most hotels have an arrangement with a local doctor who will be on-call for any problem. Each major town on the island has a hospital; however, the nearest hospital to Ocho Rios is at St Ann's Bay, and the closest to Negril is at Savanna-la-Mar.

Always take out comprehensive insurance when you travel to cover unforeseen health emergencies or accidents.

HITCHHIKING

On an island where many families do not own transport (particularly in rural areas), you will find many local people asking for and offering lifts. However, local people are not accustomed to tourists asking for lifts, and hitchhiking in Jamaica carries the same risks as in any other destination.

HOLIDAYS

Government offices and services are generally closed on the following days:
New Year's Day (1 January)
Ash Wednesday
Good Friday
Easter Monday
Labour Day (23 May)
Emancipation Day (1 August)
Independence Day (6 August)
National Heroes Day (third Monday in October)
Christmas Day (25 December)
Boxing Day (26 December)

L

LANGUAGE

English is the official language of Jamaica and is spoken by everyone on the island. However, the local population also uses a

Caribbean-English creole language when speaking with each other. It originally developed when the Elizabethan English of the British colonists mixed with the West African languages spoken by the African slaves transported to the island. With subsequent additions of English, African, and Spanish vocabulary, Jamaican English has evolved into an everyday medium that is difficult for outsiders to understand.

M

MAPS

The best road map of Jamaica, with inset detailed maps of the major towns and resort areas, is published by Shell and is available at large gas/petrol stations.

MEDIA

Radio and television. Jamaica has three TV stations and 10 radio stations, some of which are owned by the government. There are also a number of independent local radio stations, each of which operates only in a limited area. Most hotels and many bars also receive satellite services, so you'll find BBC World, CNN and ESPN widely available.

Newspapers and magazines. The major national newspapers in Jamaica are the *Daily Gleaner* and the *Jamaica Observer*, alongside *The Star*, an evening paper, *Sunday Gleaner* and the *Sunday Herald*. All newspapers can be bought at newsagents or from roadside vendors in towns. Foreign newspapers and magazines can be found in larger hotels, at the airports and at some duty-free shops in the major resort areas.

MONEY

Currency. The currency of Jamaica is the Jamaican dollar (colloquially called the 'jay'), and there are 100 cents in each dollar. Paper bills are issued in denominations of $1, $2, $20, $50, $100 and $500; coins are issued in denominations of 10 cents, 20 cents, 50 cents, $1 and $5. The smaller coins, being practically worthless, are being phased out. The US dollar is also widely accepted in shops and restaurants.

Jamaican dollars may be converted to foreign currency at the airport before departure upon presentation of an official exchange receipt. If you intend to arrive or leave with more than US$10,000 or J$150,000, you must declare this to Jamaican Customs.

Travellers' cheques and credit cards. Travellers' cheques are widely accepted in Jamaica for cash in banks, for goods in shops, and for hotel and restaurant charges. Credit cards are also widely accepted except for fuel purchases, which must be made with cash (Jamaican or US dollars). If you want to obtain a cash advance with a credit card, you must take your card into a bank and produce photo ID. There are an increasing number of ATMs (cash machines) in Jamaica, accepting a variety of international credit and debit cards.

Currency exchange. Money is changed at hotels, though at a less advantageous rate than in banks. There are also a number of 'Cambio' shops which are official money changers. You must have one official exchange receipt if you want to change money back before you return home. Changing money on the black market is illegal, but it is one of the services offered by street merchants. Beware of being cheated if you decide to use these unofficial money changers.

OPENING TIMES

Banks: 9am–2pm Monday to Thursday; 9am–4pm Friday.
Business offices (including Tourist Board): 8.30am–4.30pm, Monday to Friday.

Shops: 9am–5pm Monday to Saturday, but this can vary enormously in resort towns and from low to high season.
Museums and galleries: 10am–5pm Monday to Saturday, but private 'great houses' and plantations are open daily.

P

POLICE

Police officers wear navy uniforms with red stripes on the hat and trousers. The emergency phone number for the police is **119**.

POST OFFICES

All major towns have a Post Office. These are open 8am–5pm Monday to Friday. The postal system is notoriously slow, and postcards often take three weeks to reach their destination. If you have anything important or urgent to send, it is best to use a commercial carrier.

PUBLIC TRANSPORT

The metropolitan areas of Kingston and Montego Bay have an improved bus system. Taxis and bus franchises provide easy commuting to coastal and interior areas of the island.

The tour company JUTA *(see page 118)* operates commercial air-conditioned bus services between the airports and the major resort areas. As an example, a one-way trip from Sangster Airport at Montego Bay to Negril costs around US$25.

Once you are settled, many restaurants and bars will provide free transportation in the evenings if you eat with them; just give them a call from your hotel. Taxis are plentiful, but remember to use cars with red number plates: these are registered and properly insured. Always agree on a price for the ride before you get into the taxi, as they do not carry meters. Find out from other travellers what the going rate is for the journey that you want to make.

R

RELIGION

Jamaica is a Christian island, with Protestant denominations in the majority. However, many other major religions are also represented and have places of worship. Contact the Tourist Board *(see page 124)* for details about church services.

One of the significant religious minorities is the Rastafarian movement, whose true adherents are said to number fewer than 100,000. With their characteristic dreadlocked hair, they are seen as being almost synonymous with the image of Jamaica. Their influence on the popular culture of the island remains strong.

T

TELEPHONES

Local calls. When in Jamaica, you need dial only the seven-digit local number; there are no area codes within Jamaica.

There is a network of public telephones on Jamaica. The smaller settlements rely on them as a means of communication. Public phones, especially in the resort areas, take phone cards; others only take coins. Phone cards are available from hotels, banks and shops. Coin-operated phones will take money after the connection has been made.

The digital direct-dial system on the island is prone to glitches. Many larger hotels will have direct-dial but will charge a premium for calls made. Smaller hotels will allow calls from the reception telephone but will also charge a premium for the service.

Long distance. When calling from abroad, the country code for Jamaica is 876. When making an international call from Jamaica, always dial 00 before the country code. Some frequently dialled international codes are as follows: US 1, Canada 1, UK 44, Ireland 353, South Africa 27, New Zealand 64, Australia 61.

TIME ZONES

Jamaica operates on Eastern Standard Time, which is 5 hours behind GMT; however, it does not switch to daylight saving time. The following chart shows the time in various cities in winter:

Los Angeles	New York	**Jamaica**	London	Sydney
9am	noon	**noon**	5pm	4am (next day)

TIPPING

Tipping is standard practice throughout the island, except at a few all-inclusive resorts where the 'no tipping' policy is clearly stated. It is common for a service charge to be automatically added to restaurant bills; this should be clearly stated on the menu or on the bill. If not, then a 10 percent to 15 percent tip should be added.

For taxi drivers, tip 10 percent to 15 percent; for porters, J$10 per bag; for hotel maids, J$100 per day.

TOILETS

There are very few public toilets on Jamaica. Use toilets in hotels and restaurants or at attractions before setting out on journeys.

TOURIST INFORMATION

For useful information to help you plan your trip, the Jamaica Tourist Board has offices in the following countries:

US: 5201 Blue Lagoon Drive, Suite 670, Miami, FL 33126 tel: (305) 665-0557; 1-800-233-4582 (toll-free); email: info@visitjamaica-usa.com.

UK: 1–2 Prince Consort Road, London SW7 2BZ, England, tel: (020) 7225-9090; email: mail@visitjamaica. uk.com.

Canada: 303 Eglinton Avenue East, Suite 200, Toronto, Ontario M4P 1L3, tel: (416) 482-7850, 1-800-465-2624 (toll free); email: jtb@visitjamaica-ca.com.

There are several ways to obtain tourist information when you are on the island. The official website is www.visitjamaica.com.

Tourist Offices can be found in the following locations:

Kingston: 64 Knutsford Boulevard, P.O. Box 360, Kingston 5, tel: 929-9200; e-mail: info@visitjamaica.com.

Montego Bay: at Cornwall Beach, P.O. Box 67, Gloucester Avenue, Montego Bay, tel: 952-4425.

Port Antonio: City Centre Plaza, P.O. Box 151, Port Antonio, tel: 993-3051.

W

WEBSITES AND INTERNET CAFÉS

A number of websites can provide you with information about Jamaica before you book your trip, including details about hotels and attractions, car rental companies, and general facts and history:

www.visitjamaica.com – official site of the Jamaica Tourist Board

www.whatsonjamaica.com – weekly entertainment and sport guide

www.jamaica.com

www.go-jamaica.com

All these sites will link you with other useful sites for your trip. In addition, individual hotel websites and e-mail addresses have been added to the 'Hotels and Restaurants' section at the end of this book.

Jamaica has clusters of internet cafés, which are widely available in the tourist areas. Many of the larger hotels also offer the use of a computer in a public area or WiFi internet access for visitors who travel with their own laptop.

Y

YOUTH HOSTELS

There are no youth hostels in Jamaica.

Recommended Hotels

In both style and price, there is a wide choice of accommodation in Jamaica. At the upper end of the scale are the large, expensive luxury resorts and boutique hotels offering exclusivity, which are popular with honeymooners and celebrities. There is also a range of standard hotels at all levels. More modest accommodation can be found in small guesthouses and family-run hotels that offer clean rooms but few other facilities. A few historic plantation houses have been converted into hotels for a 'colonial feel'. Whatever your budget and taste, there will be something on the island to suit you.

Jamaica pioneered the all-inclusive hotel, where all your meals, drinks, sporting activities and other services are included in the price. This is the bedrock of mass market tourism on the island. Most of the resorts are in the north coast beach areas of Negril, Montego Bay and Ocho Rios. Some specialise in family holidays, others are for couples only. The resort chains have locations across the island, check their websites for details: Beaches, www.couples.com; Decameron, www.decameron.com; Iberostar, www.iberostar.com; Riu, www.riu.com; Sandals, www.sandals.com; Sunset Resorts, www.sunsetresortsjamaica.com; SuperClubs, www.superclubs.com.

The following selection of hotels covers a variety of accommodation options. The categories below indicate prices in US dollars per room, based on double occupancy.

$$$$	over $200
$$$	$150–200
$$	$100–150
$	under $100

MONTEGO BAY

Coyaba Beach Resort and Club $$$$ *Mahoe Bay, Ironshore (8km/5 miles east of Montego Bay), tel: 953-9150, 877-232-3224 (toll-free from US and Canada), www.coyabaresortjamaica.com.* Plantation-style rooms with hand-carved furniture, satellite television, 'silent' air conditioning, ceiling fans, hairdryers, in-room safes. Private white-sand beach, swimming pool, heated jacuzzi and a private dock with pick-up for fishing and diving charters. Complimentary water sports including sailing, windsurfing, kayaking, pedal boats and snorkelling. Land-based activities include a children's playground, tennis courts with visiting professional coach, gym and massage. 50 rooms including junior suites, some are connecting; no kitchenettes. Three restaurants.

Gloustershire Hotel $$ *Gloucester Avenue, Montego Bay, tel: 952-4420, www.gloustershire.com.* On the 'Hip Strip', opposite Doctor's Cave Beach, with bars, restaurants and clubs within walking distance; casual and welcoming. 95 rooms and junior suites, tiled floors, air conditioned, nicely decorated, garden or ocean view, some with balconies. Buffet breakfast with Jamaican and American specialities; restaurant and separate café.

Half Moon Golf, Tennis and Beach Club $$$$ *Rose Hall, Montego Bay, tel: 953-2211, www.halfmoon.com.* Beautifully landscaped gardens and a private bay giving the resort its name. Set in 160 hectares (400 acres) of grounds, with 34 villas, 152 suites and 46 rooms, the hotel has been a luxury destination since 1954. Mahogany furniture, Jamaican paintings, cable TV, air conditioning, mini-bars, hair dryers and in-room safes. The resort has six restaurants, a variety of snack bars, a spa and a shopping village. Land and water sports facilities include squash, tennis, health and fitness centre, equestrian centre and a par-72 championship golf course.

Ridgeway Guest House $ *34 Queen's Drive, Montego Bay, tel: 952-2709, www.ridgewayguesthouse.com.* A small, family-run inn with 10 simple rooms in a modern block, built in the garden of the original guest house and within walking distance of the airport. The staff are friendly and can help to arrange excursions, car hire is available on site. Good value accommodation.

Round Hill Hotel and Villas $$$$ *John Pringle Drive, Montego Bay, tel: 956-7050, www.roundhilljamaica.com.* A casually elegant hotel set in a former pineapple plantation, with seaside freshwater pool and opportunities for snorkelling in the crystal clear waters of a private white-sand beach. Well-equipped exercise room, tennis courts, yoga; varied nightly entertainment including a beach bonfire picnic with lively calypso tunes and dancing. 38 ocean-front rooms designed by Ralph Lauren and 74 suites in 27 individually owned villas.

The Tryall Club $$$$ *20km (12 miles) west of Montego Bay, tel: 956-5660, 800-238-5290 (toll-free from US), www.tryallclub.com.* A luxurious seaside villa hideaway with a championship golf course on a 890-hectare (2,200-acre) tropical estate, originally a sugar plantation until 1918 when coconut palms were planted. Presided over by a Georgian great house and situated in manicured gardens and rolling hills, with 2.5km (1½ miles) of coastline and a palm-dotted white sand beach. Privately owned villas with 2–8 bedrooms.

Wexford $$–$$$ *39 Gloucester Avenue, Montego Bay, tel: 952-2854, www.thewexfordhotel.com.* Convenient for nightlife and the 'Hip Strip', just across the road from the public beach. Renovated and redecorated in 2007, rooms and one-bedroom apartments, sea view or garden view overlooking the pool. Tiled floors, air conditioning, TV, phone, balconies, a good option if you want to be in town. Shuttle service and free entry to Aquasol Beach. 60 rooms.

RUNAWAY BAY

Club Ambiance $$–$$$ *Main Road, St Ann, Runaway Bay, tel: 973-6167, www.clubambiance.com.* Large all-inclusive resort with 100 rooms in five blocks. All rooms have air conditioning and a sea view. There is also a refurbished three-bedroom, private beach-front villa available to rent. Three beaches, one is clothes optional. Nightclub, restaurant and shops on the complex. No guests under 18 years old.

Tamarind Tree Hotel $–$$$ *Runaway Bay, tel: 973-5490, www.tamarindtreehotel.com.* A short distance from Runaway Bay and the beach, this resort has 25 simple but comfortable rooms and three villas available for rent. Pool, bar and wireless internet access for guests, and there are also several good restaurants within walking distance.

OCHO RIOS AND ENVIRONS

Goldeneye $$$$ *Oracabessa, St Mary, tel: 975-3354, www.golden eyehotel.com.* An exclusive and luxurious retreat created around the former home of James Bond author, Ian Fleming. The resort, which is part of the Island Outpost boutique hotel chain, has a main house with three bedrooms, and a growing number of private villas dotted around the property. Accommodation is tastefully decorated and there is access to the beach and water sports.

Hibiscus Lodge $$ *83–87 Main Street, Ocho Rios, tel: 974-2676, fax: 974-1874, www.hibiscusjamaica.com.* Rooms perched on top of cliffs surrounded by gardens, with paths and stairways down to the sea, but no beach. The reef just offshore is good for snorkelling. Located a short way out of the centre of Ocho Rios, but within walking distance of the shops and nightlife. The hotel has a good restaurant on site and a bar overlooking the water. Good-sized swimming pool and cliff-top jacuzzi. 26 simple rooms with air conditioning and fans, balconies have a sea view; you pay for the pretty setting rather than the amenities, but good value for Ocho Rios.

Jamaica Inn $$$$ *1 Old Road, Ocho Rios, tel: 974-2514, www. jamaicainn.com.* This has been one of the island's best hotels since the 1950s, with 47 suites overlooking a lovely, private beach. This award-winning hotel offers excellent amenities and personal service; it is beautifully designed and maintained. Luxury facilities include spa treatments and delicious local cuisine.

The Little Pub's Inn $ *59 Main Street, Ocho Rios, tel: 974-2324.* An unusual two-storey Georgian building five minutes from the beach, The Little Pub is a centrally located complex with restaurants, shops and a cocktail bar with a resident band. All 25 rooms in the Inn have air conditioning (some with loft) and cable TV. A good budget option with friendly service. No pool.

Rooms Resort $ *Main Street, Ocho Rios, tel: 467-8737, www. superclubs.com.* A budget option from the SuperClubs chain. 99 rooms in a three-storey beachfront block near the centre of Ocho

Rios. Simple air-conditioned rooms. Facilities include kayaking, windsurfing, snorkelling and scuba diving, and there is a pool on the property. Breakfast only. There is also a branch in Negril.

Royal Plantation $$$$ *Main Street, Ocho Rios, tel: 974-5601, www.royalplantation.com.* Seafront resort in operation since the 1950s, with 77 suites, an award-winning restaurant, spa, watersports, scuba diving and little luxuries such as 24-hour room service, beach butler and afternoon tea. Revamped bedrooms have comfortable down mattresses and Italian sheets on the mahogany beds, as well as conveniences such as a mini bar, data port and TV. Guests also have access to the exclusive Upton Golf and Country Club, with complimentary transport to and from the 18-hole championship course.

PORT ANTONIO AND THE EAST

Blue Lagoon Villas $$$$ *Blue Lagoon, Port Antonio, tel: 978-6245, www.bluelagoonvillas.com.* Luxurious sophistication next to the Blue Lagoon. You can reach four white-sand beaches, four restaurants, five bars and an island by taking a boat or simply diving from your villa's deck and swimming to them. Complimentary access to Frenchman's Cove beach. 13 villas with 1–4 bedrooms, fully staffed, with airport pick-up for guests.

Great Huts $ *Boston Bay, tel: 353-3388, www.greathuts.com.* Located on the cliffs of Boston Bay this beachfront eco-resort is perfect for a romantic weekend or a holiday with the whole family. Accommodation is in rustic African-style bamboo huts, treehouses and tents. Some units have hot water, some share bathrooms and all have electricity. Surfing, snorkelling and yoga facilities. The price includes breakfast and WiFi internet access; restaurant on the property. The Boston Jerk Centre is nearby.

Frenchman's Cove Bed & Breakfast $$$–$$$$ *Frenchman's Cove, Portland, tel: 993 7270, www.frenchmans-cove-resort.com.* In a beautiful location on an 18-hectare (45-acre) private estate outside Port Antonio, with a white sand beach and freshwater stream. Simply decorated villas of varying sizes set on cliff sides. This long-established resort is slightly dated but quiet and relaxing. Facilities include a grill and two bars.

Goblin Hill Villas at San San $$$–$$$$ *San San, tel: 925-8108, www.goblinhillvillas.com.* A lush site set high on a hillside with excellent views over the sea. Self-contained villas of one or two bedrooms with fully equipped kitchens staffed with cook/housekeeper. Freshwater swimming pool and two tennis courts. Complimentary access to San San beach and Frenchman's Cove; nature trails lead through the gardens with extensive lawns and woods.

Jamaica Palace Hotel $$$–$$$$ *Williamsfield, tel: 993-7720, www.jamaica-palacehotel.com.* Large comfortable hotel with slightly dated decor. 80 suites and rooms with air conditioning and bath/shower. Also on the property are an art gallery, a swimming pool and a good restaurant.

Mocking Bird Hill Hotel $$$$ *Port Antonio, tel: 993-7267, www.hotelmockingbirdhill.com.* On a hilltop above the town, five minutes' drive from Frenchman's Cove beach. A tranquil hideaway nestled in the verdant foothills of the Blue Mountains, decorated throughout with original art and with an art gallery attached. The hotel promotes environmental awareness, encouraging sustainable development at all levels. The hotel is popular with birdwatchers. Fine restaurant. White-tiled rooms with Jamaican hand-crafted bamboo furniture and locally printed fabrics offer a garden view downstairs; superior rooms upstairs with views of the hillside and the sea beyond.

Strawberry Fields Together! $–$$ *Robin's Bay, St Mary, tel: 999-7169, www.strawberryfieldstogether.com.* Formerly the Sonrise Beach Retreat, the secluded and rustic cottages sleep 35 dorm-style or 7–8 couples. There is also a camping area with bamboo hut and tent rental. Quiet during the week but busy at weekends with Jamaican families staying over or just here for the day. Private beach with life guard, snorkelling, volleyball, trampoline, table tennis and organised excursions. Meal plans available; local cuisine.

THE BLUE MOUNTAINS

Forres Park Guest House $–$$ *Mavis Bank, tel: 927-8275.* Entrance on the main road by the Mavis Bank Coffee Factory, rooms are available in the main house or in nearby cabins on the working coffee farm. Trails for hiking and birdwatching, although most of the birds can be seen at daybreak from the balcony. Guides can be arranged for a trip to Blue Mountain Peak. Spa treatments will rejuvenate you after your excursions.

Lime Tree Farm $$$$ *Tower Hill, Mavis Bank, tel: 881-8788; www.limetreefarm.com.* Three cottages on a working coffee farm with views of the Blue Mountains and surrounding valleys. Large bedrooms, bathroom and terrace, spacious enough for a small family. Price includes transfers from Kingston and all meals. Delicious food using local ingredients and herbs. Good hiking and birdwatching.

KINGSTON AREA

Christar Villas $$–$$$$ *99-A Hope Road, Kingston 6, tel: 978-3933, www.christarvillashotel.com.* Minutes away from the financial district of New Kingston and the Bob Marley Museum. Each studio and apartment in this gated complex offers air conditioning, TV, telephone, wireless internet access and a fully equipped kitchenette. Swimming pool and fitness room, business centre, restaurant and sports bar.

Indies Hotel $ *5 Holborn Road, Kingston 10, tel: 926-2952, www.indieshotel.com.* 15 rather small rooms in two wings overlooking a patio garden. Single, double and triple rooms available, all with bathroom, air conditioning, cable TV and phone. Simple but adequate with good, budget-priced restaurant and bar. Convenient for shops, restaurants, entertainment and sightseeing.

The Jamaica Pegasus $$$–$$$$ *81 Knutsford Boulevard, Kingston 5, tel: 920-4040, www.jamaicapegasus.com.* Situated in the financial and business district, close to many of the area's foremost attractions. All rooms are equipped with high-speed internet access, satellite TV, hair dryers, safes, electronic locks, complimentary coffee- and tea-making facilities, at least two telephones in the bedroom and balconies with either mountain or pool/ocean view. Non-smoking floors. Restaurants and cafés offer a variety of fare, plus there are bars and evening entertainment. 350 rooms.

Morgan's Harbour Hotel $$–$$$$ *Port Royal, tel: 967-8040, www.morgansharbour.com.* Situated in Port Royal at the entrance to Kingston Harbour, with commanding views of the city skyline and the Blue Mountains. Spacious accommodation, which was renovated after Hurricane Ivan in 2004. Each room has satellite TV; freshwater swimming pool, small private beach, complete with scuba and water sports centre. Dining is in the acclaimed restaurant next to the yacht marina, which provides some excellent evening views. With transfers from the airport, this is a convenient place to stay if you arrive by air at night.

Strawberry Hill Hotel $$$$ *Irish Town, St Andrew's, tel: 944-8400, www.strawberryhillresort.com.* Romantic, delightful cottages feature traditional 19th-century Jamaican architecture for an authentic colonial atmosphere. Near Kingston and surrounded by the Blue Mountains and 10 hectares (26 acres) of extensive gardens, with exceptional panoramic views (including Kingston) and an infinity pool, small but perfect. In-room CD and DVD players with selection of music. Excellent fusion cuisine. Spa treatments, yoga pavilion, plunge pool and sauna encourage health and well-being. The hotel, part of the Island Outpost chain, has won many awards for its architecture and design, and is one of the best places to stay in the whole of the Caribbean.

TREASURE BEACH (SOUTH COAST)

Ital-Rest Cottages $ *Treasure Beach, tel: 421-8909, http://italrest. com.* Two simple, rustic, thatched cottages with a mountain or sea view, each with two bedrooms, two bathrooms and kitchen. The café in the garden has music, dominoes and table tennis. Local restaurant close by. Friendly and helpful, 100m/yds to the sea, this is genuine laid-back Jamaica.

Jake's $$–$$$$ *Calabash Bay, Treasure Beach, tel: 965-3000, 960-8134, www.jakeshotel.com.* An eclectic collection of colourful cottages set atop low cliffs in a secluded bay, and a truly special place to stay. Created by theatrical designer Sally Henzell and part of the Island Outpost chain. Each room has a different theme, from Jamaican shack to Mexican pueblo and they vary in size from a single room with a garden view to a 4-bedroom cottage, including delightful, romantic honeymoon suites. All have in-room music equipment and free use of the hotel's extensive music collection. Tropical ceiling fans and mosquito nets maintain the traditional feel. Freshwater, rock-lined swimming pool; excellent restaurant with the freshest of seafood and other local specialities.

Sunset Resort $$$–$$$$ *Calabash Bay, Treasure Beach, St Elizabeth, tel: 965-0143, www.sunsetresort.com.* 14 rooms and suites overlook Calabash bay and beach where there are fishing boats pulled up on the sand. American and Jamaican-owned, it is good for family groups as suites can become apartments, and large parties can rent the entire villa. Staff can arrange deep-sea fishing in traditional boats or motor cruisers. Rather odd green astroturf around the pool. Satellite TV, air conditioning, coffee makers, flowery wall decorations.

NEGRIL

The Caves $$$$ *Lighthouse Road, West End, tel: 946-1958, www.thecavesresort.com.* Part of the Island Outpost hotel chain, this award-winning romantic hotel is perched on the cliffs above the sea. Luxury cottages of thatched wood and stone. Inside the caves are an intimate dining room and part of the spa. Steps lead down to the water where you can snorkel in more caves. Relax with a yoga class or explore the area on bicycles, kayaks or rafts. Wedding and honeymoon packages available. No children under 16.

Charela Inn $$$–$$$$ *Norman Manley Boulevard, Negril, tel: 957-4277, www.charela.com.* Forty-nine rooms on the beach in a long-established, family-run hotel with Jamaican-French owners and French chef, so food is a priority. There is a bakery in the hotel and they have one of the best wine lists on the island. Rooms vary in size and amenities but are well-equipped and three are adapted for wheelchair users.

Rockhouse Hotel $$$$ *West End, Negril, tel: 957-4373, www. rockhousehotel.com.* Commanding a rocky promontory in West End with views of spectacular sunsets, this collection of thatch-roofed villas has a tranquil setting. Cliff-top pool and access to swimming and snorkelling in Pristine Cove more than make up for the lack of a sandy beach. Not suitable for young children. 34 rooms, studios and villas.

Seasplash Resort $$–$$$$ *Norman Manley Boulevard, tel: 957-4041, www.seasplash.com.* On the narrow part of Negril's 11-km (7-mile) sandy beach, within walking distance of beach bars and restaurants. Rooms and suites are spacious and comfortable, with good fittings and furnishings, all well equipped. Low-season prices drop by one-third from high-season rates and are excellent value, it is least expensive May to June. Very good restaurant on site, Norma's On The Beach, with steps down to the sea.

Tensing Pen $$$–$$$$ *West End, Negril, tel: 957-0387, www. tensingpen.com.* 16 luxurious rooms in cottages perched on cliffs with hammocks and lots of private areas for quiet sunbathing and relaxation around the property. Laid back, unpretentious and sociable. Yoga and massage facilities on site. Breakfast is included and dinner is served five nights a week, but there's a wonderful kitchen with a sea view for all to use and enjoy. Wedding packages available. Tensing is the guard dog.

Xtabi Resort $–$$$$ *Lighthouse Road, West End, Negril, tel: 957-4336, www.xtabi-negril.com.* Eight seafront cottages, or rooms in cottages, in tropical gardens on the cliffs offer a choice of simple or luxury accommodation. Steps lead down to caves for snorkelling. Native wood floors and rustic furnishings, outside showers with privacy walls. All rooms have safes, some have kitchenettes and many have refrigerators; the garden rooms are more modern, with tiled floors and air-conditioning. 24 rooms.

Recommended Restaurants

Jamaica offers a wide range of restaurants, offering both local and international cuisine. Most of the larger resort hotels have acclaimed dining rooms that are open to the public. There are also many independent establishments with a high reputation and a faithful clientele.

Reservations are frequently necessary in the high season. In the off season, reservations are appreciated at all times but should definitely be made at weekends. Some of the more expensive establishments have a dress code; you should enquire when you make your reservation. Many restaurants will offer free transport from and to your hotel when you make a booking.

Unless otherwise indicated, all listed restaurants offer breakfast, lunch and dinner daily. The following price categories indicate the approximate cost of a three-course meal, per person, excluding drinks; tips are extra. Prices are in US dollars:

$$$$	over $50
$$$	$30–50
$$	$20–30
$	under $20

MONTEGO BAY

Houseboat Grill $$$–$$$$ *Southern Cross Boulevard, Montego Bay, tel: 979-8845.* Restaurant on a houseboat moored in the Marine Park close to the Freeport, reached by a short pontoon ride. Dinner only, with the bar open from 4.30pm for sunset drinks. Mostly steak and seafood but they also offer excellent vegetarian options. A glass-bottomed section is fascinating for children – there are lots of fish around, including tarpon and snook.

Margaritaville $–$$ *Gloucester Avenue, Montego Bay, tel: 952-4777.* Lively sports bar and grill located at the start of the main strip. Roof-top deck with water chute and floating trampoline. Frequent 'special' evenings with themed entertainment. Free pick-up service. More formal (and more expensive) dining at Marguerite's next door.

The Native $$–$$$ *29 Gloucester Avenue, Montego Bay, tel: 979-2769.* A romantic, open-air restaurant with international and local dishes on the menu. Look out for the sweet dumplings, smoked marlin and spicy chicken. All-you-can-eat buffet at weekends. Open for lunch and dinner.

The Pelican $$$ *Gloucester Avenue, Montego Bay, tel: 952-3171.* Long established local favourite that is popular with visitors too. Hearty Jamaican food, including a good breakfast menu, and American specialities. Good value for money.

The Pork Pit $ *27 Gloucester Avenue, Montego Bay, tel: 940-3008, 971-5375.* Very basic but very good Jamaican food – jerk chicken, pork and ribs sold by weight, served through the kitchen window, with garden gazebos to sit and eat in. Cash only.

Scotchie's $ *Coral Gardens Villas, Rose Hall, Montego Bay, tel: 953-3301.* Casual dining near the Holiday Inn. Open 11am–11pm, serving some of the best jerk pork, chicken and fish with local accompaniments such as roasted breadfruit, potato, yam or festival.

Tapas $$$ *Cornice Road, off Gloucester Avenue, Montego Bay, tel: 952-2988.* Elegant veranda dining on hillside above Gloucester Avenue. Music adds to the ambience and the stylish presentation of European and Middle Eastern cuisine with a touch of Jamaican flavouring. Dinner only, from morning until night. Major credit cards.

RUNAWAY BAY

Ultimate Jerk Centre $$–$$$ *Main Street, Runaway Bay, tel: 973-2054.* A casual, popular roadside restaurant serving tasty, affordable and authentic Jamaican food. Theme nights one weekend a month.

OCHO RIOS

Almond Tree $$$$ *Hibiscus Lodge Hotel, Main Street, Ocho Rios, tel: 974-2813.* A gourmet restaurant offering great views of the sea and serving international and local cuisine. Inside and open-air dining by candlelight.

Evita's Italian Restaurant $$$$ *Eden Bower Road, Ocho Rios, tel: 974-2333, 974-1012, 974-1718.* Italian food with a touch of Jamaican spice. The essential place to see-and-be-seen, this is the only restaurant overlooking both Ocho Rios and the sea. Everyone in the music, fashion, or film business has probably eaten here. Lunch and dinner daily from 11am–11pm.

The Little Pub $$–$$$ *59 Main Street, Ocho Rios, tel: 974-2324, 974-5825.* A complex of cocktail bars and restaurants offering live music six nights a week along with the ubiquitous karaoke and large-screen satellite TV. Menus comprise a mixture of Jamaican specialities as well as American and European dishes in a lively – and noisy – setting.

PORT ANTONIO

Anna Banana's $$ *7 Folly Road, Port Antonio, tel: 715-6533.* A small beach-side restaurant and sports bar located a little way out of the town centre. Decent Jamaican cuisine with seafood specialities and good value for money.

Dickie's Best Kept Secret $$$–$$$$ *Port Antonio western outskirts, tel: 809-6276.* An unassuming painted shack on a clifftop overlooking the bay, run for many decades by Dickie Butler, who is rumoured to have entertained Errol Flynn, Princess Margaret and Winnie Mandela, among others. Reservations only, but you can eat breakfast, lunch and high tea here. Excellent home cooking and quite an experience.

Mille Fleurs $$$ *Hotel Mocking Bird Hill, Port Antonio, tel: 993-7267.* A creative mix of international and local cuisine that includes a good vegetarian selection. Most produce is locally grown, with some from the restaurant's own organic garden. Located in a beautiful position in the foothills of the Blue Mountains offering spectacular panoramic views. Dinner only, daily 7–10pm.

BLUE MOUNTAINS

The Gap Café $$–$$$ *Hardwar Gap, Newcastle, tel: 997-3032.* High up in the hills with wonderful views over Kingston, this 19th-century way station is an ideal place to stop when hiking or touring the Blue Mountains. Open for breakfast, lunch and high tea, with delicious Blue Mountain coffee. Jamaican and Italian food, from curry goat to pizza, or combine the cuisines with jerk chicken pasta. Indoor or outdoor dining, with elegant china and table linen in the restaurant.

KINGSTON

Bullseye $$$ *Knutsford Boulevard, Kingston, tel: 960-8724, 960-8609, 960-8723.* Steaks to please the most discerning palates, plus an excellent salad bar with plenty of choice; this simple and straightforward combination is difficult to beat. Lunch and dinner daily, 10am–10pm.

Cuddy'z $$–$$$ *Shops 4–6, New Kingston Shopping Centre, Kingston, tel: 920-8956.* Owned by former West Indies bowler Courtney Walsh, this sports bar is popular with sports personalities and the after-work crowd. Friday night is lively with scheduled events. Jamaican and international food or TexMex, lots of choice.

Jade Garden $$$ *106 Hope Road, Sovereign Centre, Kingston, tel: 978-3476, 978-3479.* Hong Kong chefs prepare traditional Chinese food and the island's two largest saltwater tanks ensure that all seafood is absolutely fresh. There is a choice of over 100 dishes. Views of the Blue Mountains from picture windows are spectacular. Reservations recommended.

Up on the Roof $$–$$$ *Knutsford Boulevard, Kingston, tel: 929-8033.* Indoor or outdoor dining on the roof, Caribbean as well as local specialities; excellent food with several vegetarian options and an assortment of salads. Open Monday to Friday noon to midnight, Saturday 6.30pm–midnight; on the last Sunday of each month, there is an evening theme party from 5pm.

TREASURE BEACH (SOUTH COAST)

Jake's $$–$$$$ *Jake's resort, Calabash Bay, Treasure Beach, tel: 526-2428.* The best of Jamaica's spicy cuisine, including saltfish and ackee, rice and peas, fish in coconut milk and escoveitch fish. The catch is always fresh. Soups include conch chowder, cream of pumpkin, red pea with pieces of beef and yam and pepper pot.

Little Ochie $–$$ *Alligator Pond Beach, tel: 965-4449.* Great setting on the beach with wooden tables under thatch, some made from old fishing boats on stilts. Choose your own fish, lobster or other seafood, have it cooked to order and served with bammy, festival and scotch bonnet chillies (these can be very hot).

Yabba $$$ *Treasure Beach Hotel, Treasure Beach, tel: 965-0110, 965-0114.* Jamaican and international cuisine, including fresh seafood, served in a relaxing atmosphere. The vegetables are grown on the owner's farm. Open for breakfast, lunch and dinner.

NEGRIL

Errol's Sunset Café and Guesthouse $–$$ *Norman Manley Boulevard, Negril, tel: 898-0400, 957-3312.* Located right on the beach, this is an ideal place to spend some time having lunch or a sunset drink. An excellent menu of Jamaican meals is offered, especially the selection of fresh soups, at very reasonable prices. It's not the place to go if you are on a tight schedule, as all the meals are cooked individually to ensure their freshness, but it's great place to be while you wait. Cash only.

Gambino's $$$ *The Beachcomber Club, Negril, tel: 957-4170.* Casually elegant outdoor dining with an ocean view. All the usual Jamaican favourites, along with authentic Italian food. Buffet and à la carte available. Free pick-up service.

Hungry Lion $$–$$$ *Lighthouse Road, West End, Negril, tel: 957-4486.* Lunch downstairs, dinner upstairs on the roof terrace or indoors. Healthy, natural foods in an arts and crafts ambience.

Just Natural Restaurant $$ *West End Road, Negril.* Excellent vegetarian meals from appetizers to desserts, prepared to perfection. Also offers fresh fish. Particularly good for authentic Jamaican breakfast with a huge fruit plate.

Kuyaba $$ *Norman Manley Boulevard, Negril, tel: 957-4318.* Caribbean and international cuisine set amid tropical foliage and indigenous architecture. There is full beach service during the day and a happy hour from 4.30pm until the sun goes down. Free pick-up service.

Margaritaville Bar and Grill $$–$$$ *Norman Manley Boulevard, Negril, tel: 957-4467.* Lively sports bar and grill located centrally on Negril's beach. Convenient for lounging on the beach, with full service available. Frequent 'special' evenings with themed entertainment. Free pick-up service.

Norma's $$$$ *Sea Splash Resort, Negril, tel: 957-4041.* Restaurant by the water with a romantic atmosphere. European cuisine with a Jamaican nouvelle flair. Open for dinner.

Rick's Café $$–$$$$ *West End, Negril, tel: 457-0380.* Open for lunch and dinner offering everything from surf 'n' turf to chip 'n' dips. Rebuilt after Hurricane Ivan in 2004, but still the place to come for sunset watching with local lads diving into the sea from rocks and trees for tips. Live music during the evenings; a lively, happening place.

Treehouse Restaurant $$$$ *Norman Manley Boulevard, Negril, tel: 957-4287.* Imaginative Jamaican cuisine. The menu includes chicken, pork, fish and seafood cooked any way you like, pizza also features. Sunday jazz and breakfast on the beach. Open for lunch and dinner.

Xtabi Cliff Restaurant $$–$$$ *Xtabi Resort, Lighthouse Road, Negril, tel: 957-4336.* This place is justly proud of its lobster and meat dishes, chargrilled or cooked any way you like. Cliff-top location overlooking the sea.

INDEX

Berlitz pocket guide

Jamaica

Sixth Edition 2008

Written by Jack Altman
Updated by Sarah Cameron
Edited by Lesley Gordon
Series Editor: Tony Halliday

Photography credits
Alamy 57, 61; Pete Bennett 14, 17, 30, 35, 37, 65, 84, 87, 90; Kevin Cummins 6, 8, 9, 11, 12, 22, 26, 28, 29, 31, 32, 33, 38, 39, 41, 42, 43, 44, 45, 47, 49, 50, 51, 52, 53, 54, 55, 63, 64, 66, 67, 69, 70, 71, 73, 74, 75, 76, 77, 79, 80, 82, 86, 88, 89, 91, 92, 94, 95, 96, 99; istockphoto 59, 101, 102, 104, 105; Photoshot 24; 15, 19, 21 The Jamaica National Library.

Cover picture: jonarnoldimages

Printed in Singapore by Insight Print Services (Pte) Ltd, 38 Joo Koon Road, Singapore 628990. Tel: (65) 6865-1600. Fax: (65) 6861-6438

Berlitz Trademark Reg. U.S. Patent Office and other countries. Marca Registrada

Every effort has been made to provide accurate information in this publication, but changes are inevitable. The publisher cannot be responsible for any resulting loss, inconvenience or injury.

Contact us

At Berlitz we strive to keep our guides as accurate and up to date as possible, but if you find anything that has changed, or if you have any suggestions on ways to improve this guide, then we would be delighted to hear from you.

Berlitz Publishing, PO Box 7910, London SE1 1WE, England.
fax: (44) 20 7403 0290
email: berlitz@apaguide.co.uk
www.berlitzpublishing.com